Anyone who has heard Abbé Pierre speak will recognize his words and the very tones of his voice in this book. In the Introduction he indicates his experiences as child, boy, curate helping Jews to escape from the Gestapo, patriot in the underground, member of Parliament. The large, dilapidated house first called Emmaus he rented and began to repair with the idea of making it a youth centre. One day he found a homeless man, who in despair had tried to commit suicide, and said, "Come and help me," thus saving him by enlisting him in the service of others.

This was his first contact with the utterly destitute, and it made him realize that a man may be long "blind and senseless" without being heartless.

Educated in a well-off family, Abbé Pierre himself had never even heard, what he has since become, "the voice of the voiceless." Families came to Emmaus who had nowhere to live; he filled the house, bought and re-erected old huts, bought land and material, was helped by an increasing number of poor men who ransacked garbage cans for usable items. These ragpickers had housed one hundred and forty-one families before the Abbé's radio appeal to the French nation brought wider support.

In his talk to young seminarians Abbé Pierre begs these future priests to be haunted by the sufferings of the world. The poor man needs not a program, not a plan, just food and a home. But the politician finds it impossible to imagine the condition of the homeless. In a world where babies die of cold quite legally — but are kept alive illegally if you have not the necessary building permits — the Prophet must return, standing in poverty near God and proclaiming God's judgment on human indifference.

To convert the poor you must be like them, to convert the rich you must be unlike them.

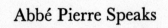

Abbé Pierre Speaks

Le pouvoir est fait
non pour servir le plaisir des heureux
mais pour la délivrance
de ceux qui souffrent injustement.

Abbé Pierre

ABBE PIERRE SPEAKS

Speeches Collected by L. C. Repland

*Translated by Cecily Hastings
and George Lamb*

SHEED & WARD - NEW YORK

Nihil obstat:

BARRY E. FONTAINE
Censor delegatus

Imprimatur:

✠ EDWARD F. RYAN, D.D.
Bishop of Burlington

July 7, 1956

CONTENTS

CONTENTS

ILLUSTRATIONS

"But before all things have a constant mutual charity among yourselves: for charity covereth a multitude of sins. . . .

". . . as every man hath received grace, ministering the same one to another. . . .

". . . If any man speak, let him speak as the words of God. . . ."

THE FIRST EPISTLE OF ST. PETER THE APOSTLE,
Chapter IV.

"Let us never lose our living conviction that it is not necessary to wait
until we are splendid people
before we can do splendid things
—that would probably mean waiting a long time, too long in fact!
We only need to understand
one splendid thing
and then try
to base our whole life on it:
and that thing is
that the first person we must help
in all things
is the person who is suffering the most."

(From the RULE OF LIFE OF THE
COMPANIONS OF EMMAUS)

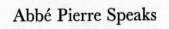

Abbé Pierre Speaks

INTRODUCTION

SAYING YES WITH THE LORD

Well, it's certainly an excellent question to ask—however an ordinary little fellow like me became a priest! But it's so difficult to answer. And it doesn't make it any easier, asking the priest to answer for himself: in fact, perhaps it only makes it more difficult.

Where in fact in the whole vast range of human life can you find a more mysterious thread of events than that which goes to make a priest? On the one hand there is the all-powerful and yet infinitely gentle freedom of God Himself, and on the other the highly precarious freedom, swaddled in darkness and imperfect as it is—and yet at the same time crucial, since nothing can have any value without it—of the child of man who finally accepts this vocation, involving as it does both sacrificing and being sacrificed.

There can be no doubt that, as to what happens while these two freedoms make their way towards each other, the times of joy and misery, enlightenment and fear, the *"in manus tuas commendo spiritum meum"* that follows upon the *"Eloi, Eloi, lama sabbachthani"*—things always involved when the creature turns to his Creator—no one can ever know anything of importance save the person himself, for such knowledge can

1

only come through direct experience, and the experience is always unique. There can be no doubt that the only person who can know about these things is the person who has lived through them. And when it is a matter of trying to tell others about them, as distinct from simply knowing them oneself, there is a kind of impossibility about it. Again, there can be no doubt that we all have very little idea of the real, if relative, importance of each of those moments that have turned us from what we were into what we are, made us the voice and hands of God. And then again, what are we now, compared with what we shall be, when we finally come to the beginning of all perfection, finally grow into the bliss of Heaven, when finally the time comes for us to receive that blessing above all blessings—the absolute certainty of never again being able to destroy anything, being utterly in love with Love, caught into the life of Love that joins Father and Son and Holy Spirit, being not only out of the range of sin but beyond even the possibility of sinning, in that state of infinite perfection when we can no longer do evil but live for ever like Jesus and Our Blessed Lady?

We should have to be in Heaven before we could answer your question. And then how marvellous it will be when we are able to see right into each other's souls, and see that facet of Himself which our Lord has stamped like a star upon every single one of those who through His grace have persevered until the hour of full enlightenment came, persevered in longing and repentance and service!

Despite the fact that you know all this, and know that it is impossible for anyone to answer your excellent question, you have asked some of us to try to answer it. And we must certainly forgive you for this and try to do what you ask. For you may be right, for however little we may be able to make out what has happened, and pass it on to others, that little, even though it may not get beyond the abc stage, will still be there on one of these pages, and we may be no more than the poor parchment, but the hand that writes it will have been God's. And, possibly, this may cause something to awaken in someone, and yet another person will be prepared to make an offering of himself to God.

And the entire human world has such a tremendous need for this kind of offering that it is really only suffering because not enough of them have been made. The suffering is absolutely frightful, from one end of the world to the other, and it is ultimately the same suffering everywhere.

How could anyone possibly refuse to do all he can to accord with God's will to go on, right to the very end of the world, to the time of the new beginning that has no end, creating a sufficient number of us, God's priests, through whom He brings salvation!

When I reflect on how I became a priest, and think back as far as I can to when and where the germ of the desire to be a priest first appeared, and when I had my first inkling of the great adventure to come, I seem to see that the whole thing began with a shock I received when I was about five years of age. I can remember this almost down to the minutest details. It was one time when my father got very angry with me. My parents were comfortably off: they had eight children and I was the fifth. On this particular day—it was a Thursday—I had done something very silly indeed and they told me that I was to stay at home in the afternoon while my brothers and sisters went off to a big children's party at some cousins' of mine. And so it was. In the evening they all came back in a state of great excitement and started telling me what a wonderful time they had had. I have never forgotten this episode, even though I was so small at the time. In an abrupt, sulky voice I said, "What do you think I care? I wasn't there!"

and stalked off. My father was some distance away, but he
heard what I said and took me aside, and I could see that
though he was usually so good-tempered, he was deeply out-
raged and very angry. He said that it was absolutely abominable to talk like that, and that God hated that kind of selfish-
ness; and he went on talking to me for a very long time. When
he finally left me to myself I felt absolutely bowled over. For
I had had a very strong sense of not having behaved naughtily
in any way, not having done anything wrong, of being perfectly logical in my attitude to the whole thing, and this had
given me a sort of satisfaction. I had felt that my behaviour
had had a kind of frigid perfection about it. And for a long,
long time I thought about not only my father's explanations
and feelings in the matter, but—and it was the opening of a
new world to me—his passion, the genuine suffering that had
been revealed to me through his words, from which it had
been quite clear, as his indignation showed, that the deepest
depths of his being had risen up in real unhappiness against
the contemptuous attitude I had adopted. And this was perhaps for me the real practical beginning of the discovery of
the joy that lies in giving others happiness, even to the extent
of depriving oneself. Of course my mother and everyone else
in the house had often told me about the value of sacrifice,
etc.; but that day brought me a dramatic personal discovery.
The fact that so many tiny details connected with it should
have remained scored on my mind for nearly forty years
makes it seem fairly certain that it was all of a piece with the
other decisive events that gradually fashioned my life. How
can I ever thank my father enough for having been the kind
of person he was, so that my misguided words made him
tremble with passion, so that my heart, and not simply a cold
and deceptive semblance of reason, opened to his meaning!

Assuredly family prayers, which were said every night without fail, played a great part in my early life too. Time and again since I have become a priest I have been able to fall back on this personal experience and urge anyone who wants to be the head of a genuinely Christian family to give his children this most precious of all lessons and heritages, the sight of mother and father going down on their knees daily in humble, fervent prayer to God, so that the children can see the people who order them about all day presenting themselves in their turn to God just like children themselves, and examining their own consciences in silence. People who have never had the good fortune to have their childish sensibility struck by the sight of this kneeling in prayer can never really understand what a wonderful thing it is.

Perhaps two little things that happened when I was a child were also important for the future.

One day when I must have been about eight some relative or other took me and another little boy for a walk, and, I forget why, this person happened to say, "It's such a lovely thing to be a priest, wouldn't you like to be one?" My companion replied that he would. I was absolutely dumbfounded by this: I had never given a thought to what I was going to be when I grew up, but this fellow had not only thought about it but had even decided to become a priest! I felt a sort of wonder at this, but all I said was, "I don't know." . . . Today that little chap is a married man, the father of a large family, and the whole family is a model of what a Christian family should be. I'm the one who became the priest! That's the way God's plans work out. . . .

That seems to have been the first day that I ever realised that every priest had once been a child like me.

A little later, probably when I was about ten—and here

again the details are astonishingly vivid—I was in a tram in some seaside town during the holidays. I was with a number of other children and a lady was with us. She started talking about one of her uncles, who was a missionary somewhere or other, a long way away. We all listened entranced. And then again the same question was put to each of us: "What are you going to be when you grow up?" It came to my turn to reply, and I can see myself, half-boastful, half-triumphant, announcing, "I'm going to be a sailor or a missionary or a bandit!"

When I was in the *maquis* I was hunted like a bandit for two years. Then I was for two years a chaplain in the navy. And I have been through a good deal of missionary territory in Africa; while my work as a priest, which is now amongst the very poorest people in the country, is surely very close to missionary work, isn't it?

So when the time comes for me to die I shall be just like a spoilt child who has had everything he wanted. May the Lord not judge me too severely for the unsatisfactory way I have responded to such spoiling!

When I got back from this holiday—I had seen the sea for the first time—I was haunted by the idea of the missions. I began to read about them and find out everything I could about them.

One night in the following year—I must have been eleven —when my father came in to say goodnight to me, my day's homework being finished, I announced, "Daddy, I have a big secret to tell you: I want to be a priest." A very long silence followed these words. Finally my father gave me a great hug and said, "You know, that will cost your mother and me an awful lot, old chap—but we should be very proud of you." And he went away. He never referred to the secret avowal again until the day came when at the age of eighteen, after many periods of crisis, I told him that I wanted to go off and become a novice with the Capuchins.

Not long after the secret avowal, I decided to become a scout. Scouting often reveals deficiencies in later life in people who have not had the kind of education it gives corrected and perfected by realities of a harsher kind; nevertheless it provides a marvellous training for growing boys. I could never say how many graces I received from being a scout during those few years.

When I was about thirteen a lengthy crisis slowly began to develop in a highly unusual way.

I was ill for several months and took to reading everything I could lay my hands on. One day it happened to be Descartes, and his *Discourse on Method* and the rule about whole numbers threw me with a blinding flash into the astonishing cerebral world of pure logic, the first suspicion of whose attraction I had really experienced when I was five.

Two years later, during a Sunday morning religious lesson being given by a priest, a remarkable man, at the Jesuit College in Lyons where I did all my schooling, a "clear idea" suddenly flattened me out with its brutal clarity. "Here you are," I thought, "living according to this Faith of yours; but suppose you had been born anywhere else, amongst Mahomedans, for instance, or in India, or just amongst people with no religion at all, and supposing you had made no greater personal effort than you have made so far, to criticise and substantiate what you have been taught to believe, then obviously you would believe things to be true that you now believe to be false. Well, then, how can you be sure that what you now base your way of living on, and tomorrow will base your actual life on, is true?" I was absolutely bowled over. The thought brought a great void with it, but also the feeling that there was a passionate battle waiting to be waged.

My health was precarious, and I was given all kinds of privileges. When the spring came I often used to go and spend lesson time alone in the Place Bellecour, which is quite close to the school. There I would hurry through my Latin prose or my essay and then go browsing through old books and take masses of notes. I still have a pile of old exercise books dating from those days. There were some dark and bitter hours.

This period was dominated by three decisive influences. The first was occasioned by the reading of a bit of Kant, and rather more of Hegel, and anything I could find by contemporary writers on the various philosophies of becoming. It is difficult to explain to anyone who has not experienced it the kind of intoxication that can take possession of the mind under the influence of any sort of pantheistic idea. It has a confused sort of tang and strongly tempts one to fall back into an effortless possession of infinity, as I myself experienced at this time.

But during this same period circumstances which it would take too long to explain led me to read first St. Teresa of the Child Jesus's *Story of a Soul,* then, one after the other, Joergensen's life of St. Francis of Assisi and the *Fioretti.*

Then there followed nearly a year during which I was again ill for most of the time, and I began to pray differently from the way I had prayed in the past—anxiously.

One day I happened to be reading something whose title I can never remember, when I came to a page where the author is describing the way the Lord appeared to Moses, who had asked Him, "Who art thou?" And the answer had come: *"Ego sum qui sum—*Yahweh."

That was undoubtedly the most decisive day in my whole life.

Later, during the years spent in studying theology and the spiritual life, I was to gain a better understanding of the mysterious relationships that form the essence of the Eternal One in His Trinity of Persons, the Eternal, Unchanging Life that knows no shadow of contradiction, but it was on the day I came across that passage that I experienced this as a fact, and with a certainty which in the twenty-five years that have followed since has never known a moment's doubt (and how can I ever be humble and fearful and at the same time trusting enough towards God to be able to thank Him for it!).

After years in which thought and inner life had been obscurely seeking their way simply by considering the movement and becoming of everything, this idea of Essential Being was like a rock or block, and coming across it by chance, as I did, my whole being and personality and faith fastened upon it unshakeably.

Thank you, my God.

Since then I have suffered much and in many different ways, as all who follow You must suffer, Lord, but from the suffering of doubt, never. Oh, how I pray that to those whom You choose to bring to Yourself through this form of suffering, in the unfathomable but loving decisions of Your will, You may grant that they may go through the various stages from communion to the redemption of the world and ascend to Your light! Have pity on their pain, shed Your light into the anguish of their doubting hearts, You who are only dark to our minds because, like the sun to our earthly eyes, You are excess of light! Enter sometimes into the eyes of those who suffer, that they may see!

A few months later I was beginning my novitiate with the Capuchins in the Lyons province. It was almost easy.

The years when I was studying theology, on the other hand,

were terrible, harder than I can ever describe, and my health declined rapidly. However, I managed to get through them.

And by St. Bartholomew's Day, 1938, I was a priest.

The trial which had been preparing for years brought, in the following year, a decision of a very cruel kind. Just before Easter I broke off the extra year's theology that I was doing at my own request and, on the advice of my spiritual director, left the monastery relieved of my vows by the Holy See. A few weeks later, after a retreat at the Trappist house at Aiguebelle, I was accepted by the diocese of Grenoble the week after Easter and became assistant priest in a big parish in the town.

And this was the beginning of that whole sequence of events that has turned Abbé Pierre into the poor fellow so many people talk about, and who can apparently do nothing to stop it! And who knows that being a celebrity is the most encumbering thing there is! And who, faced by all the world's manifold miseries, often gives way to the temptation to murmur to himself, "Quickly, bring time to an end! Things as they are are too frightful!" but who quickly stifles any such outburst because he hopes for an increase in the number of people who, faced with the paroxysms of pride and greed and stupidity caused by human passions, and with such dangers as leave our proudest national leaders dumb and helpless, come to realise that today a great task awaits them, one which they really can do, and which calls upon every clear-thinking mind and generous heart for its fulfilment: the task of devoting oneself utterly to proving to all the people of the earth that when Christians say that all men are brothers and equal sons of God, these are not simply fine words but mean that we really are prepared to help others—feeding the hungry, finding houses for the homeless so that they don't have to live like beasts of

the field, finding them proper work so that they can earn their
daily bread in a decent human way, and providing schools
and hospitals so that they may teach their children and tend
their sick. Then there will be fewer blasphemies, and perhaps
hope of a less poisoned peace in the world.

Six months after I had begun my work as an assistant priest,
the war of 1939 broke out. I was invalided out of the army
after rather more than a year's convalescence, and was called
to Grenoble Cathedral, as assistant priest again, helping Jews
who were being hunted down by the Gestapo. This was the
beginning of many a frontier crossing! Then followed the
creation of the tragic, heroic *maquis* in Chartreuse and
Vercors—to whom I was also chaplain—which was made up
of people who refused to submit to the abominable compulsion
of being sent to work in German war factories.

I was arrested twice, escaped, was in Africa by the end of
1944, then chaplain in the navy, then on another two months'
mission through darkest Africa, and as soon as I got back
went into Parliament. . . . And while with the money I got
from being a deputy I was starting the first "Emmaus" venture for men whose conditions were absolutely desperate, then
the first little "city" of homeless working-class families, I decided to get out of Parliament rather than bow to an unjust
law. . . . All that remains is simply the story of the increasing growth of the "Emmaus" venture and its increasing
acclaim by the public, all leading to the immense burdens that
have to be borne today.

If in the course of these over-long pages I have spent so
much time describing my fifteen years of wanderings as a
priest pitchforked into such unexpected kinds of work, it is
because I should like all of you, my friends, who are now
doing your studies in theological colleges, and suffering—for

in theological colleges particularly, maturity must come
through suffering—to have the benefit of my own experience.
Listen and believe what I say, believe it absolutely, and let it
be a source of endlessly renewed patience to you: I am certain
that if I have been able to get through so much danger and
such times of exhaustion, seemingly beyond all human en-
durance, without giving way, without becoming spiritually
dried up and lost in spite of so many sins and failures, it is
because of what slowly developed during the long years of
theological study—the habit of prayer, which creates a network of power-lines, of simple but powerful bonds with God.
No one can foresee what ordinary or extraordinary way he
will be called upon to follow as a priest, but you all know
that all the roads that priests tread lead up to Calvary, where
side by side stand the Cross, the sign of an excruciating death,
and the empty tomb that signifies resurrection. Oh, arm yourselves with patience, so that the harder you find these years in
college, the greater and stronger your hope may be. You are
the chosen stones whom the mighty Workman is knocking into
shape for His cathedral, and from each stone He expects its
own especial beauty, as slowly, with His seeming cruelty, He
digs and chips away at it to turn it into a work of art that is
one single hymn of praise.

And however different the sculptures and aisles and vaults
may be, a single cathedral begins to emerge here, finally growing by an invisible but eternally marvellous process into the
Kingdom of God.

All we are asked to do is to say "yes," not on our own, but
with God.

All we are asked to do is to make perfect our will, and—
clutching on tightly to the rope tearing our hands—to keep
our sail taut in the wind.

The wind is the breath of Love, the Eternal One, the Spirit proceeding as a unity from the Father and the Son. It never stops blowing. No one knows where it comes from or where it is going to, but It knows. And because it is "He," "He" who "is," the One and the All, that gives us ground enough for hope.

May our Blessed Lady who was the first person ever to put herself entirely at His disposal, correct us, fortify us, and smile upon us—Our Lady who now looks down upon us from a region beyond all shadow.

Abbé Pierre

Emmaus, September 26th, 1954
Feast of Our Lady of Mercy

RADIO—"THE LAST QUARTER
OF AN HOUR"*

THE WORLD IS JUDGED BY POVERTY

Man is only truly himself when he tries to discover the
essence of his own existence, an existence which he has not
willed and which he suddenly wakes one day to find himself
in.

If I had to sum up in a final message what I have been led
to regard as the essence of this life of ours, I think that I
should first of all, before passing on my message, wish to be
sure that I was speaking to all the different categories of our
human brothers. For—and are we sufficiently aware of this?
—these different categories live in such different (such terribly
different) conditions, that it is almost impossible to address
them all at once. Speaking to one of them sometimes even
seems to make it impossible for one to be understood by any
of the others. We are cut off from each other by too many
differences of suffering.

I think that first of all those of my brothers to whom I
should primarily wish to speak are those who are in despair,
in despair with that most terrible of all despairs, which is

---

* Paris, April 16, 1954.

15

caused by the sense of guilt one may labour under from a consciousness of having perhaps done wrong, but which is almost always accompanied by a very acute consciousness of the fact that though one may have done wrong it is not fair for one to be made to suffer to such a terrible degree and be utterly abandoned through the hypocrisy of others. Yes, indeed, it is to these most desperate ones that I should like to speak first, and say: Whether you are guilty or not, if you have really been reduced to a condition in which you feel absolutely annihilated, and have a sense of being quite outside all human fellowship and human society, then I want you to know and believe that nothing is lost ultimately, because there is a form of justice of an absolutely complete and faultless kind, and the day is coming when, provided that you have simply known how to love, have known how to look upon the sufferings endured by those around you, you will come to know what the prophet of old was not afraid to call "vengeance," the vengeance that comes from the Eternal One. . . . The last shall be first, so long and so soon as they have been able to get beyond their own sufferings and love others.

I should like then to go on to speak to the kind of people who are not actually desperate but who are on the way to becoming so, not actually desperate because they have not lost all their means, have not yet been absolutely ground down and reduced to a state of powder but nevertheless feel hounded and crushed by the official mechanisms of the societies to which they belong.

Well, to these people I should like to be able to say: Learn to unite and to turn your eyes, and the strength you gain from uniting, not first of all towards the people above you, but towards those who are less fortunate than yourselves. And putting this strength at the service of your less fortunate brethren, save yourselves and others too, and by saving others, the most desperate ones of all, you will hurl a stone of scandal in amongst the fortunate ones, the privileged ones, and this may mean that they will all take a closer look at themselves, and many of them may change their ways and begin to develop an interest in that love that begins as a hunger and a thirst for justice.

This struggle undertaken by the suffering, uniting to save those who suffer even more and hurling their defiance at all the people who are comfortably off, is I believe the really essential thing to be done, as a matter of reason and also as a matter of Christian faith.

Then, finally, I should also like to be able to say a word to those others of my brethren whom God also wills to save, and whom He in fact finds it most difficult of all to save, the people who are comfortably off, or seem to be comfortably off, people who suffer from that worst of all errors, self-satisfaction.

To these people, then, who hold the power, who are safe, or imagine they are safe, because they are well educated, because luck has always been on their side, because they know the right people, to these people I should like to be able to say: Please, for your own sakes, open your eyes before it is too late! Don't you realise that all your different kinds of culture are artificial, are all under a curse. They are artificial because the only things they teach you to regard as being of any value are things that are successful from the human point of view; they tell you all about masterpieces of art, literature, science; they tell you all about historical or military glory, as it is called, the great resources of your national heritage, but the thing that all these different kinds of culture have forgotten, or have made a systematic resolve to keep you in ignorance of, is the relativity of all these values. And all these different kinds of culture are under a curse so long as they bear this mark of artificiality and duplicity, so long as they are not accompanied by some kind of co-efficient to show what a tiny proportion of mankind has any chance of enjoying these precious values and works of art. How many are there amongst you, the kind of people I was brought up amongst and belonged to for so long, how many of us are there who, despite the fact that we may have the most remarkable qualifications and the most exceptional abilities and are brainy people with the most brilliant intellects, have no sort of concrete practical knowledge of the fact that this very day, when we are enjoying all our cultural refinements, three out of every four people alive on this earth have not had enough to eat—today, at this very moment—to grow up into normal adult human beings? That today, on this earth, every other family that exists is without the absolute minimum of living space that it needs to live a decent family life in conditions above those of beasts? That more than half the children born into the world exist in conditions in which they have to suffer to a degree beyond the imagination of people like us who have everything we want? I should like to be able to say to these people: How many of you realise that at this present moment a mere ten per cent of the human race, people like us, are quite heartlessly wasting more than eighty per cent of the wealth and resources produced by the earth today—and it would produce a good deal more if talent and genius and power and material and moral energy were all devoted, not to a continual increase in the comfort and convenience of those who are comfortably off, but were really, fiercely, passionately, put at the service of, devoted to the help of, the great mass of mankind that is wasting away.

To these people, the comfortably off, I should like to say: Before it is too late, wake up, let us all wake up, for in point of fact you—we—will be judged and condemned by the poverty we have disdained as beneath our notice.

The world is judged by its poverty—judged in time and judged in eternity; and we are all judged according to the attitude we have adopted towards it. God created the world, and at the centre of it placed that marvel, man, and each man, according to the power he wields in this world, is directly responsible for the worldly success or failure of the great mass of his brethren.

In actual fact, the law of life that we all have to discover and acknowledge is that all societies and all individuals live or perish according to whether they realise that it is the person who has to suffer the most who is to be put first. No one who has not realised this—has not realised the absolute right possessed by the person who has the most to suffer to be served first—is properly speaking a human being. And no nation is truly human unless it has understood this too. This is an absolutely fundamental law, the law by which we as Christians believe that God Himself willed to become the Son of man, willed to identify Himself with those who suffer the most, to the point of being born in a manger in the straw, and then die between two criminals, rejected by His own people and the people in authority.

The law of the universe is that one must love one's neighbour as oneself, but this is no more than a hollow mockery unless it means putting the less fortunate members of the human race before oneself. It's not true that we love our neighbour as ourselves until we put the less fortunate ones amongst us before ourselves.

May many people come to realise this throughout the whole world! Then and then alone shall we be able to say that there is some hope of peace without seeming to be either misguided or stupid, because then and then alone the kingdom of love will have come into existence—that love which is only genuine when it begins as a search for justice.

Men who stand erect are glad to call themselves Emmaus workers.

Every Sunday morning there is a Community Meeting.

TALKS IN VARIOUS TOWNS IN FRANCE, BELGIUM, AND SWITZERLAND*

FACING UP TO DESPAIR

Friends,

What am I to talk about this evening?

I think the first thing you should realise is that the people who have been involved in this venture of ours, not only since the first of February but for a number of years now, and who now find people in all kinds of distress coming to them in a state of extraordinary hope, are in a way more bowed down with burdens than ever before.

It is so heart-breaking to have crowds of people coming to see you, in a state of suffering which they have done nothing to deserve, and to realise when you are faced with this overpowering flood of human beings that you are in point of fact unable to give them the help they expect from you. It is very hard to bear.

To be able to conquer this feeling, we all need to have a great deal of tenacity, a great deal of wisdom and method, a

---

* February to October, 1954.

21

great deal of intelligence. It needs a great deal of personal initiative from each particular individual, but at the same time it needs organisation and co-ordination. It is not enough to expect everything from a mere handful of people who have happened to hit the limelight in a rather melodramatic way. These people can suggest ideas and new lines of development, but how can you possibly expect them to solve all the problems they are faced with, on their own? This can only be achieved if everybody joins in, if in every district in our own town, in every town in France, and in every country in the world, everybody does something about it on the spot.

If this evening is to be of any real use and have any real effect and not be simply an excuse for a lot of enthusiasm and fine feelings, and excitement about a few people regarded as stars, as though they were some kind of trapeze artists in a circus—which would be a great pity!—each of you must come to see what it is all about.

A REVOLT AGAINST ABSURDITY

Very well then, what is it all about?

What is really involved is, I believe, something going far beyond the outer shell of the events that have taken place during this winter in France and given the country such a severe shaking-up—and not only in France but the whole world, for we keep getting letters from all over the place, telling us of changes of heart that have taken place as a result of the events of this winter.

Often when people speak about these events they describe them as a sudden outburst of human kindness.

It is quite true that the events have included a formidable amount of human kindness, but it is also true that the events have not only been a matter of kindness. In the first place there was an outburst of intelligence and a protest against an absurd condition of things. Fundamentally it meant the end of a nightmare, a nightmare of shame for a whole people who had been condemned to live like idiots when they knew that they were not idiots.

When young children happen to die in a catastrophe that takes place somewhere on the earth's surface, through the flooding of the dykes as in Holland, or an earthquake like the one in Greece, or the floods in India, when a catastrophe of this kind occurs, it is cruel and terrible and frightful to have to see so many innocent people lose all the fruits of their labours, but, when we have done all we can to help them and show them that we are their friends, what we always say is, "It is nobody's fault, of course."

On the other hand, when in a country like France little children of working-class families—decent working folk, people who are not vagabonds or idlers—die of cold or hunger, when in the streets of Paris old men who have spent their whole lives at decent honest work die of cold, we have a deep feeling—and we need to have this feeling, right deep down inside us—that it is all very cruel and horrible and frightful, but something far worse as well, because it is in fact idiotic, because this kind of thing is happening in a country in which, as we very well know, if things were organised from the heart with courage and intelligence, such horrors would be quite unthinkable.

That is the way we felt and it was against such an absurd condition of things that France in fact rose up as a whole in one great urgent movement, not only of kindness but also of anger and protest, and said, "What can we do as a body to stop this immediately, and give our own working men enough decent living space to enable them to come back home from work and find their wives and children living in houses fit for human habitation?" It is fair to say that what lay behind the movement that spread over the whole country was a kind of determination to ensure that such stupid horrors should never be seen again.

THE RESURRECTION OF A PEOPLE

It can be said that it was in a way a kind of national resurrection, for France was in a state resembling that of a corpse. What is a corpse? Is it something which has lost all its life? By no means. A corpse is full of all kinds of life, swarming with myriads of lives. But there is something missing to make it a living body: it lacks a common soul, a central soul, to co-ordinate all its conflicting aims and all the various lives that make up the rich harmony of a living body. It lacks a central soul to bring the whole organism into unison with itself.

France was like a corpse. There was no lack of life in it. It too was swarming with life—life of all kinds, all full of their own dynamism, but what was lacking amongst us, amongst all those human beings who had to live together in the same country, was a single idea, a single subject on which we could all agree, on which we could all be unanimous.

What took place on February the first was truly the rebirth of a common soul, the resurrection of a joint will to prevent innocent people from suffering in such a stupid way.

And that is what we must come to realise this evening.

THE HORROR OF THE WORLD'S POVERTY

Do you realise, friends, that whilst we are sitting here with all our privileges behind us—privileges that have enabled us to grow up into educated cultured people, and to develop our capacity for enjoying things of beauty—do you realise that at this very moment, over the whole face of the globe, there are masses and masses of people living in conditions which it is no exaggeration to describe as hellish?

Do you realise that more than half the world's inhabitants —and this has been proved by the latest scientific reports to the United Nations—have nowhere to live—and in this connection, somewhere to live simply means a place where man and wife can retire and be alone in a way worthy of their human dignity and not like beasts in a stable?

Do you realise that at this very moment, when privileged people like us have more food on our tables than we can eat, three quarters of the earth's inhabitants have not enough rice or corn to enable them to go on living and grow up into healthy adults?

Do you realise that there are vast regions of the earth's surface where three out of every four children die of hunger before reaching adolescence?

This morning I was talking to a friend of mine who has just come back from a world tour. He has been in countries in which the responsible authorities told him that they had decided to stop vaccinating young children and not to do anything to prevent them from dying because they knew that they had not enough food for them to live on. So they had decided quite coolly, as a matter of political necessity, not to give these children any of the benefits of science, or try to help them to

avoid catching any mortal illness, because they would rather
see them carried off by an epidemic than have their mothers
bringing them to them in crowds because they have nothing in
the way of milk or soup to give them!

THE AGONY OF FRENCH LIVING CONDITIONS

Do you realise, friends, that at this present moment throughout the whole of France there are more than three hundred
thousand families, according to the most optimistic estimate,
whose members do not know where they will be sleeping
tonight, don't know whether they will be taking shelter in
cellars or barns or sleeping two or three families in the same
room, with hundreds and hundreds of them out of doors? In
the Paris area alone there are more than ten thousand families,
that is to say about one hundred thousand people, who don't
know where they are going to sleep tonight, and of whom it
can be said that if they are not found a minimum of living
space within the next few months, there will be broken homes,
whole families in despair, and children either in want or
abandoned.

That is the situation.

We have to realise—because it is the truth—that Western
Germany alone—I have no statistics about the rest of that
country—built more than half a million houses last year,
whereas we only built a quarter of that number.

We have to realise that of all the nations of Europe France
comes right at the bottom of the list as regards the number of
houses built per thousand of the population.

Are we going to let this state of affairs last any longer?

We must make up our minds to change all this, because
the country that calmly accepts it is a country under a curse,

a ruined country. That is what we have to realise. When three quarters of a nation's inhabitants are comfortably housed and they take not the slightest interest in the rest who have no roof over their heads, then that country is a country of savages, not a country of civilised people. It certainly cannot be called a Christian country.

We must understand that we deserve to have a curse on us so long as we fail to grasp the gravity of the problem.

It is all one vast tragedy.

To bring it to an end, to heal this wound that exists in France, we need the energy of every single person. Public opinion, that is to say we—you and I—have to become aware of the problem. We have to get angry about it, we have to make sure that the people with the means—whether money, or authority, or business position, whatever means it may be— do something about it. We have to make such a nuisance of ourselves that finally they wake up and do what needs to be done.

Let us see things as they are. After all, if we were able to unite in the face of this problem and show our elected representatives—the people in authority—what we really want, if we were able to get together and order them about, they would do whatever we want them to do if only to get themselves re-elected. They would obey us, and that is what democracy means. It is up to us to open our eyes. It is up to us to become aware. It is up to us to give our orders and make our demands.

"NO-GOODS"

Sometimes people with a comfortable roof over their heads come along to me and say, "Oh, monsieur l'Abbé, how splen-

did you are, how much we all admire you—and how sorry
we are for you, because of course all these people without
anywhere to live must cause you an awful lot of disappointment. They are all more or less bound to be no-goods; they
must have something wrong with them, for all really decent
people, thrifty people, people with a bit of spirit, always manage to come out on top, don't they? But these down-and-outs
can't really be any good."

Well, friends, when people say that sort of thing to me, I
always have the same sort of answer ready. "Very true, sir,"
I say, "very true, madam! How right you are! It's quite true
that the homeless and down-and-out include people who can
be described as 'no good,' but it's also true that there are no
more of that kind of people amongst the homeless than there
are amongst the people who spend their lives in drawing-
rooms and business offices. The truth is that it's the same
humanity in both cases, the same kind of people, the same
human hearts all with their own faults and vices. No doubt
some of the down-and-outs get drunk. But I suppose there
are no people getting tight on cocktails and champagne at
the other end of the scale! The truth is that there are virtues
and vices on both sides. There are admirable, heroic people
amongst the suffering and homeless—admirable people struggling as hard as they can and yet driven to despair. If it so
happens that some of these take to drink, I am quite sure
that God will forgive them, whereas He certainly will not
forgive those who seem much less blameworthy on the surface but who in fact never offered to give these others a helping hand or a roof over their heads and so save them. Which,
in the eyes of God, will be the guilty ones?"

That is what we have to realise.

Have you ever thought of taking an honest look at one

simple fact about this world of ours, which is usually described as being divided into the free peoples and nations on the one hand and the peoples and nations who have lost their freedom on the other—a fact that, properly reflected on, will open up whole new vistas to your minds and consciences?

Have you ever thought that the broad general fact is that what are called the free nations are quite simply the nations with all the money?

The so-called oppressed nations, who have lost their freedom and are obliged to put up with this, are, generally speaking—and have we sufficiently realised this?—either poor nations, or nations left until quite recently by us and by their own rulers in conditions of the most absolute poverty.

OPPRESSION

I have had the chance to talk to so many people who have taken it upon themselves—and it is a tremendous responsibility—to become social revolutionaries in these oppressed countries! How often they have said to me—and it has been heartbreaking to listen to, for one cannot help believing that in a great number of cases they embark on this way in all sincerity, even though we know that it is a way of error, and catastrophic error at that—"How do you imagine that we could ever have got out of the poverty-stricken condition we had been left in, and sometimes systematically forced to live in, for centuries? How except by joining together and forcing upon our peoples disciplines—dreadful disciplines, but which at least gave us the hope of getting out of the appalling conditions we were obliged to live in?" I have travelled through countries in which—this is a fact—the authorities have systematically done everything they could to prevent the development of education, because they didn't want any sort of crowd psychology to develop that would lead to the making of demands or a re-arrangement of the way the money was shared out, or do anything to change the living conditions of the privileged few. Then the storm came with all its attendant horrors—which are still with us.

But, friends, it may be that at this present moment there is only one real problem as regards the future of the world, that is to say the future of the young children you care so much about and work so hard for and dream of bequeathing a happy life to—a life beautiful and holy, but at the same time happy too. Do you know that for these youngsters of the generation now growing up there is only one real problem, and that is to know what is going to happen to all those masses of people who make up half the human race, the more than a thousand million human beings living either under political oppression, or on the other hand under the oppression of hunger, unemployment, ignorance, poverty and the absence of all they need?

Your children's future does not depend on how many atomic bombs are going to be produced to defend them; it depends on our capacity—yours, mine, and the so-called free peoples'—to get outside ourselves and realise that we are cowards and poltroons if we go on leaving all these masses of people in the appalling conditions they are living in at the moment.

Your children's future depends on whether tomorrow—and I mean tomorrow—we shall be able through the pressure of public opinion to get the public authorities in our own countries to organise an immense self-sacrifice on our part so that now, at once, we can bring these masses of people, existing

all over the world's surface, what they need and will not do
without docilely for much longer. If we are not able, with
the minimum of delay, to organise—as we have managed to
organise the production of so much wealth in these countries
for our own advantage and the enrichment of our own cities,
far more than for the real happiness of the people concerned
—to organise, passionately, a certain minimum of renuncia-
tion, so as to bring at least the beginnings of sufficiency to
these people, we can be quite certain that they will determine
their own fate and future in a different way from any we
might otherwise hope to see. We can be certain that if in the
next twenty years a thousand million and more human beings
are so driven by anger and hunger that they decide to revolt,
there won't be much point in our having piled up our atomic
weapons, for there will never be enough of them to stop those
thousand million human beings, all in revolt against our self-
centredness and lack of human conscience.

THE ONE REAL MODERN PROBLEM

That is the problem that the world is facing today.

This seems to us to be shatteringly self-evident, rising up
right before our very eyes; and we feel in a way that the
phenomenal events that took place on their own small scale
last winter in our own country of France cry out that this is
the thing to be learnt, that it is our duty, a sort of God-given
mission for us, to go out and announce, as once the prophet
in Nineveh did, to all the people who take their own privileged
position for granted, "Do penance, for the day of God's
chastisement is coming, for a curse is upon future generations,
the curse that weighs upon those whose hearts have not been

big enough to open their minds and make their eyes see clearly and enable them to realise how craven it is to go on being happy when others are not so."

We must realise that the time for such craven behaviour is past, and that if we are unable to give it up of our own free will God will oblige us to give it up in some far more tragic way.

MIRACLE OR LOGIC?

It is quite true that in that month of February 1954 something extraordinary happened—just because a few words were said all of a sudden, on the spur of the moment, over the radio. They were quite ordinary words, very ordinary words indeed. When you look at them now, after the event, it all seems utterly astonishing, they are so simple. They were words that had been said a hundred times over, by people far more qualified to speak, far more important people, and yet had never before caused a ripple of interest.

What mysterious reason lies behind the fact that on this particular occasion they caused such a tidal wave of a ripple? How is it that on this particular occasion they produced an absolute storm?

The reason, I believe, is connected with a whole network of circumstances which we of the Faith describe as providential.

Oh, I know that there are some people who have been very nice to me who have found their own way of accounting for the miracle—that's to say, the journalists! I don't quite know why, but ever since that moment they have all had a frightful crush on Abbé Pierre! So, to please me, they've been writing all over the place that the true explanation is that we ought to canonise the Abbé Pierre. It's very nice of them, of course, and I don't want to upset them, but if I am to be perfectly honest I must say that I find it all slightly upsetting, because the fact is I haven't much confidence in their competence to decide on the question, and I myself prefer to leave it to God to decide, a little later on. . . .

We have to try to find the real explanation behind that sudden explosion.

So, then, what is the explanation of the storm that gave us all such a shaking up?

On reflection the explanation will be found to be as follows.

DE PROFUNDIS

When, on the first of February, we cried out in our distress and said, "Come and help us! Come and help these people who are living in such appalling conditions!" these words didn't come from on high, from people in official positions, people in authority. They didn't even come from any committee of ladies and gentlemen, possibly very fashionable, very admirable ladies and gentlemen, but the kind of people who when they are asked to help the poor talk about them as though they were looking down at them from a high balcony, because they are not themselves in the thick of it, the kind of people who say, "These people are so wretched, they must be helped," but say it from outside, from above. . . .

When that appeal was made last winter by a certain individual, it was not, for once, made from some position high above the poverty level, or by just any old person! The words that were spoken had behind them something that gave them

an extraordinary depth. They were the words of someone
speaking in the name of a queer society called "The Emmaus
Community of Ragpickers," desperate men for the most part;
would-be suicides; old lags who had come out of prison to find
that society, which in so many cases bore its own share of
responsibility for what they had done, hypocritically cast them
out and simply refused to give them anything to live by; and
others who had been driven to despair not through crime but
simply as a result of misfortune, by the war, through their
home life being destroyed because they had had to spend too
long away from it as prisoners—all these people being joined
by a few voluntary workers, simply human beings who could
no longer endure to live in comfort unless others did the same,
people who were ashamed of their own good fortune and
decided quite freely to join up with the most unfortunate
members of society and share their distress.

Yes, that appeal was made by a society of desperate men,
men who had learned to unite in their despair, to love each
other despite their faults—their undoubted faults—learned to
unite to earn their daily bread and become *men standing on
their own two feet again,* men proud of their manhood. They
had learned to unite and in thus uniting to become not simply
their own saviours but the saviours of others.

WHO ARE THE NO-GOODS?

These men—there were five of them to begin with, then
eighteen by the autumn of 1951, then, by January, 1954, two
hundred and fifty—had already by their work together managed to turn more than 110,000 individual days of misery into

110,000 days in which men lived in freedom and proudly earned the bread they ate.

These men—who had emerged from the depths of despair, from the deepest depths of poverty, *"de profundis"*—had managed by their own efforts, during the two years up to February the first, 1954, simply through their work as rag-pickers going through refuse, simply with what they had got out of their work, giving up everything that might have been due to them but the barest necessities—people who were simply, in their own words, "fair game for the cops"—these men had managed (and it was a matter of legitimate pride for them) to be instrumental in saving one hundred and forty-one working-class families.

Thus, to get down to the root of the matter, when something was said in the name of these people, it had a special, an extraordinary, kind of weight. It was something said by people who lived in wretched conditions themselves, who simply said, "Look, then, just look at what we, the no-goods, have been able to do, right on our own, on nothing, on dustbin scrapings! Just because we managed to find a little real love for each other! Well, then, understand, realise what this means! What could be done if you other people, not no-goods like us but, to take your own view of yourselves, you, the good types, joined up with us for once!"

Thus because it was a cry like that, coming from the uttermost depths of pain, the uttermost depths of suffering, it gave everybody a tremendous shaking. And that led to that extraordinary, unbelievable thing, that storm that swept over the whole country.

That, I believe, is the real explanation lying behind what happened.

Whenever big bugs say anything, there is always a tendency
—especially in a country like France, where people generally
like to show how little respect they have for authority—not to
take them seriously, a tendency to think that they have not
given much of an example themselves. But when a few words
come up from below, from the poorest, most negligible people
in the community, the people living in the most wretched
conditions, then, because we happen to be made like that,
there is a sudden upsurge of enthusiasm.

That, I believe, is the really deep point behind the story of
the Emmaus Communities of Ragpickers.

A GOSPEL EXPLOSION

And surely it contains the very lesson of the Gospels.

When Our Lord decided to do His best to move our hearts
He didn't choose to become a prince, a big bug, a high-up.
He could have done so, of course, but He knew quite well that
when a big bug comes along he can get himself feared and
even sometimes followed but he can never become the object
of that kind of utter devotion which takes possession of the
whole being.

Our Lord, who knows all the depths of the human heart,
knew that anyone who appears as a tiny child, the poorest of
tiny children, lying on straw, possessing nothing, and then
lives in suffering, hidden humbly away from the world, and
finally dies an unjust death between a couple of old criminals,
that person is capable of affecting the hardest of hearts.

Fundamentally, without any calculated intent on our part,
that, I believe, is the mysterious explanation of the formidable

shaking-up power that lay hidden in the words spoken on behalf of those communities.

Understanding is a great thing!

We were in the thick of the whole thing when we launched that appeal.

THE BEGINNING

But how had it all begun? How had it come about that we were right in the middle of the drama and able to see it and know it like that? I for my part came from a comfortable family and never in my whole life had I come across such poverty, it was something right outside my imagination. However had I got to know about it?

It was quite simple, really. You know the story already in its broad outlines: it has been told so often!

At that time I happened to be a parliamentary deputy and I was looking for somewhere to live and work. The only places I could find were ridiculously expensive and I wasn't prepared to pay the prices out of the money I got for my job. After much hunting, a day came along when I was told of a big house that was to let in the suburbs: it was supposed to be two storeys high and to have about an acre of garden complete with a couple of summer houses, and it was all going for fifty thousand francs a year! "Well, if that's the case," I said to myself—especially in view of the fact that it had been to let for a couple of years and nobody had wanted it—"there must be a snag somewhere." All the same, it was obviously a place to be seen.

I soon realised why it was going so cheaply. It was a house

that had been left derelict several years before the war and then ransacked while the war was on. The first floor was just about ready to come through the ground-floor ceiling. There were no heating facilities, no electric light. The water-pipes had holes in them. The drains were cracked and the stuff from them poured into the cellar. The outside pipes dripped all the way from the attic to the ground. Nevertheless, after a tour of inspection I decided that it was still in good shape and could be done up, and that it would be silly to let it go to ruin. So I rented it and installed myself in it at once, and I also put a family up on the ground floor, the family of one of my friends, who was a senator.

At night when I came back from the Chamber I did the house up: I was plasterer, carpenter, electrician. In my young days, when I had been a scout, they had nicknamed me "the thoughtful beaver." Fundamentally that's what I was . . . so I worked away at getting the house into proper shape. Ladies and gentlemen, if any of you are deputies now, or one day find yourselves such—it can easily happen!—I should like to give you a good tip. After a session in the Chamber, if you want to get your ideas in order, there is nothing like turning carpenter or mason and working with your hands. Anyway, the house was soon shipshape.

Then the whole thing began because the house was too big, and I didn't fancy living there like a king in his castle.

At first my only idea was to put the house at the disposal of groups of young Christians or other groups of a similar kind, and so keep in touch with them—there were many such groups who wanted somewhere near Paris which they could use on Saturdays and Sundays as a prayer or study centre or simply as a place for rest and relaxation and family outings. That was my original idea as to what to do with the house.

For some reason it was at once an enormous success. People started coming from all over the place every Sunday from our different youth groups in Paris and the surrounding districts. Before long they were coming to me and saying, "This is splendid! It answers a need. There aren't enough of these kind of houses around Paris. But it is too small. It needs to be enlarged, so that the young people can come in the evening and find themselves in a proper atmosphere of recollection the first thing in the morning."

So I went to the market and bought camp beds, mattresses, blankets, and set them up all over the house and then under canvas in the garden. The result was that we were able to put up about forty people every Saturday night.

THE EMMAUS YOUTH HOSTEL

In the beginning it was mainly for youth groups round Paris. Then in the summer it became an international centre. In point of fact the organisers of the Versailles Diocesan Works asked me to put what accommodation I had at the disposal of the Youth Centres so that it could be used by the branch of the Federation of French Youth Hostels known as the O.C.C.A.J., the Christian Organisation of Youth Camps and Hostels. I agreed, and the result was a great outburst of activity, for in the first year we had more than five thousand people from forty-one different centres spending the night there, and the next year more than seven thousand people from forty-five centres.

It was at this time that the house got its name "Emmaus."

Emmaus, as you know, is the name of a little village near Jerusalem. Well, we were in a little village on the outskirts of a capital city and we formed a sort of hostelry to take in people who were looking for God. So it was a bit like Emmaus, a bit like that inn where men in despair after the Passion and Death of Our Lord found Him again, resurrected, and set off filled with courage, transformed men no longer in fear of the police but able to go back into the city and become militant Christians like the Apostles and do their part in spreading the word of God throughout the world.

And so it was called Emmaus. We never suspected at the time that it was a far better word even than we had imagined —for the house was to become, not simply an inn, but a refuge for the absolutely desperate.

And this was not long in coming about.

THE FIRST TRAGIC MEETINGS

One day somebody came and called me out with the words, "Father, come at once, it's absolutely dreadful! There's a man in the next commune who has just tried to kill himself. He's not dead. Come at once!" I went off and saw the man. He was an old convict. He had been given a life sentence, then released after twenty years' hard labour, and had come home a few weeks before to a family tragedy so appalling that after a few weeks of it his one wish had been to die. I could see at once that there was no hope of his taking heart: he had no reason to live. This being so, it was obvious that if I left him to himself he would try and do the same thing again. So I said to him, "Listen! You are in a rotten position indeed, and I need someone to come and give me a hand. Look, I have more to do than I can manage. You come with me, and we shall be able to do some good work together." And that was how he came to the house.

He was the first of the people who found in Emmaus a source of real, new family life.

This was in 1949. And so until the day came when I got out of Parliament there were always four or five of us living on the money I got, working to put the house in order.

But as I said, people kept urging me to enlarge the place. . . .

One day I heard that the authorities were selling huts that had been built by the Germans for prisoners at the big barracks at Saint Denis. I went to the sale and bought them. I was highly delighted when I got them but my delight did not last long, for I was told that they would cost 200,000 francs* and that they had to be paid for in cash. Altogether I had 40,000. So I went to the office and told them how it was and that that was all I had; and gave them my 40,000. I always mention this as an example of how slanderous it is to say that nobody in France trusts the deputies. Because I was a deputy, I was given credit. I was given six weeks in which to pay. . . . Well, I racked my brains wondering however I was going to do it—and this led me to a line of reasoning that was at once very intelligent, very logical and very Christian. I said to myself that the Gospel tells us to love our neighbour as ourselves—and there is no better way of loving one's neighbour than by giving him a chance to do a good deed! As my nearest neighbours at the time were deputies, I went straight off to the Chamber and began tapping them one by one in the corridors.

And with the money procured in this way I managed to pay for some of the huts.

We began to take them down, carried the parts off to Neuilly-Plaisance, and put them up again. With the pergolas and rose trees they made a very nice retreat. There are dormi-

---

* Around $600.

tories containing a hundred beds, three lecture halls, a re-
fectory, kitchen, four little living rooms, and at the bottom of
the garden, the chapel, a brick chapel, in fact a bare brick
chapel, a very humble chapel indeed, with an altar made from
the trunk of an acacia tree that we felled in the garden. But
no matter how humble our chapel may be, we love it. Since it
is made of bricks bought in the way I have described, when
any of our friends come and see us and I take them to see the
chapel I always say, "Take a good look at this chapel! There
is nothing quite like it in the whole world, for in very truth
there are bricks in these walls that are praying for every political party in France." And I always go on, "There are bricks
praying for dear old President Herriot. There are others praying for the president who has just gone out. And there are
quite a lot more praying for a lot of other people, but you will
never get me to tell you their names because if I did they
would get into trouble with their parties for not being anti-
clerical enough!"

And it was in this way that, working away with three comrades of ours, we built the whole thing up to be able to accom-
modate more young people and house more down-and-outs.

And that wasn't the end of our work!

THE FIRST FAMILY

We had thus become a centre of spiritual and intellectual
life, an international meeting centre and a refuge for men in
despair.

And then a day came when this adventure took on yet
another dimension.

One day in the month of December—December 1951—

there came to us not simply one individual in his wretchedness, but a whole family—mother and father, grandfather, and three youngsters. They had been evicted. I had never come across a case of eviction before. I still had the old idea that evictions were out of date, ancient history, things that never happened in our day.

As a matter of fact I still often have people—comfortably off people—coming and saying to me, "What's that you say? Evictions? Everybody knows there are no such things! Quite impossible! I own a bit of property myself and if I wanted to take over part of it as a flat, supposing my daughter should get married for instance, well, even though theoretically I have every right to do so, I know that in fact it would be quite impossible for me to get the authorities to back me up, even though I should only be asking for my rights!"

That was my own idea until the day came along when I saw what can really happen, and ever since that day I have known that though it may be next to impossible to put out a few people who know the right people or have means, nevertheless in the case of crowds of poor souls who have no means or do not know the right people, this sort of thing is happening every day in my own district: people are being evicted.

And on that first day I really realised for the first time what eviction means. It means that people come in, forcing open the door, and the bailiffs—who are no worse as individuals than the next man, but are simply obeying orders—simply take everything—and everything means the table, for instance, any private papers there may be, all the family's things—they take the baby's cradle, they take the bedclothes, the mattress, the kitchen stove, and they throw the whole lot out on to the pavement. And then they bring in the people who have the legal right of entry!

But tell me, what about the people who have been got rid of? Suppose they are genuine working people, not wasters, suppose they are decent average people who have done everything they possibly can on the money they get, the work they do—haven't they some kind of right, a natural right in the strictest and most absolute sense, to some nook or cranny from society where they can house their children? It's far too easy to hide away behind the written law, documents, as though what is written down is the be-all and end-all of the matter. We know quite well that this is the smallest part of it, a necessary part, true, but that anterior to it there is a deeper law, a law binding upon all of us, a law that may not bring us into any of the courts where human justice is dispensed but which no one will be able to escape from when the day of judgment comes, because it is the natural law, and the law of God.

When a society has forgotten all about this law and is unable to do anything to make it generally respected, then, it must be repeated, that society has a curse on it.

GOD'S ROOM

And so we took in our first family. I had simply said to them, "You are so dreadfully miserable—come and live with us."

With us? The fact was, there was no room for them. The house had been full for a long time. I decided that the only thing to do was to put them in the little room that we were using as a chapel: it is now the kitchen. From this little room —the new chapel was still not built—I removed the altar, I removed God Himself. Instead of the altar we put in water and gas, a bed for the parents, cradles for the children. And they came and settled in.

If such marvellous things have happened since—and I often think about this—perhaps it is because we dared to do what we did. Because nobody in the town wanted to give a lodging to a homeless woman, we dared to make Our Lord Jesus Christ do it. Perhaps it was because He gave up His place to her that so many people later came to understand the position and enabled us to find somewhere to live for hundreds and thousands of families living in an anguish of misery.

THE FIRST HOMES ARE BUILT

We kept that family for a year. They arrived, as I said, in December. During the following months we put up the huts that we had bought to extend the house; then it was summertime.

In June I realised that we still had some stuff left over. This gave me an idea. I went to see this family and said to them, "What would you say if we found you a piece of land, bought it, and then with the material we've got left over we all get down to the job of building you a house?" You can imagine their reactions!

We looked about and found a miserable bit of land just by the railway bridge at Neuilly-sur-Marne station. With my deputy's money—you see how useful it can be, so don't ever say anything against it!—we bought this bit of land and set to work. By the end of four months the house was up. We had managed after much argy-bargying to get a permit to build a house of about twenty feet by eighteen: which wasn't bad. So we kept to the rules, and there was the house, twenty feet by eighteen. The only thing was that when it was finished we found that there was still some ground left, and some materials lying around, and also in the meantime more families had come along and told us what a desperate condition they were in. Well, we were so carried away by enthusiasm at all this that we used up everything that was left and the result was a house nearly seventy feet long. It had fifteen rooms in it! And five families! All done in four months—counting the buying of the land, the plumbing and the electricity for the five homes, with six feet of cellar, it had cost us 900,000 francs. True, it had only been possible because all the materials were on the spot, and all the work had been done free of charge by the community and by young helpers—from eighteen different countries—who had agreed to give a hand while they were staying at the youth hostel during the summer. But anyway by Christmas the five families were in.

Of course there were one or two bits of funny business. Somebody came along one day, for instance, and asked me to show him my building permit. I said that it was stuck up. So he said that he had seen that but it didn't quite seem to fit in from the arithmetical point of view. This led to the first of our now well-known answers in the matter of these tiffs—never very serious, I may say—with the authorities. The official in question was a very decent sort of chap and he was simply doing his duty; so I said to him, "Listen: go the whole hog and make a faithful report of what I say to you. Say that I guarantee that the four families too many will get out at once and even demolish the part of the building that is over the mark as soon as they are found somewhere else to live—and if possible somewhere better. As a matter of fact I have been told privately that there is quite a fair amount of space at the

sub-prefect's place. . . ." That was the last we heard about
that. The five families are still there. The house still stands.
We call it the "bridge house" because it is right at the end of
the railway bridge.

CATASTROPHE

But as things turned out, that house, the first we put up,
was the beginning of an absolute catastrophe, not an administrative one but one of a very different and far more terrible
kind.

In point of fact the news had immediately spread far and
wide that at Neuilly-Plaisance there were young lads and a
phenomenal priest-deputy who built houses for people who
hadn't anywhere to live, and especially for the kind of people
who know that they not only haven't got a house now, but
there can never be any question of their having one. At that
time, clearly, it was hopeless for anyone who was getting from
seventeen to eighteen thousand francs per month to imagine
that he could find anywhere to live. They all knew that, if
they did manage to find anywhere, there were always plenty
of people with more money in their pockets who would snatch
it from under their noses. If they went to the local office and
inquired about the possibility of building their own house,
what answer would they get? They would be told that certainly they would be helped, certainly they would be lent
money, but only when they actually owned a piece of land
fulfilling all the requirements and necessities of the local council's rules and also when they had at least ten per cent of the
official estimate of the cost. Now that meant, for a radius of
five to ten miles round Paris, between three hundred and three

hundred and fifty thousand francs. How many working men are there, working men between the ages of twenty and twenty-five who are married and have one or two young children, who can help blowing up when this is the sort of reply they get: "Well, yes, young fellow, when you have managed to save 350,000 out of your seventeen or eighteen thousand a week, then we, society, will always be there to give you a helping hand"? Don't you see how horrible it can be for anyone to have that said to him? Well, that was the position! There was no hope for them.

And then they heard that it was for this kind of family that houses, somewhere to live, were being built! They could see mothers and fathers coming home in the evening to decent conditions worthy of their human dignity, not living like beasts of the field huddled together in stables on top of each other, with a single room for two or three families. They could see the children's faces beginning to grow rosy.

There had been no speeches, no plans, no blueprints. We had simply built a house.

Then there began that horrible experience of crowds of human beings coming to us one after the other to tell us what dreadful conditions they were living in.

THE EXTENT OF THE DISTRESS INDESCRIBABLE

It was then that I discovered something I had never realised before. I realised that you can have a human heart and yet be utterly blind and stupid. You can live alongside people whose lives are horrible and absolutely hellish and not have the faintest idea of this because they have the decency and self-respect not to go shouting the fact from the rooftops or whining about it in the streets. They are ashamed of the conditions they have to live in. But they have to go on living in them. And they find it degrading.

I could spend the whole evening telling you about what I saw at this time, what I discovered.

One of the first of these people to arrive was a boy of twenty-five, a fine fellow, a splendid working type, proud and as solid as a rock. When he was left alone with me he began to cry like a child, and what this twenty-five-year-old lad told me was as follows. "Father," he said, "a pal of mine has sent me along to see you because they have just taken my wife away mad." And this French working man went on to describe how during their three years of married life they had been living along with two more young families in a single room, nine feet by twelve, in Montreuil. There were a couple of mattresses on wooden frames, one above the other, and another on the floor. Two babies were put in a box at the side. A third child was on the way. Three years of conjugal life, family life, in such conditions! And one of the women was mad. And this young fellow sobbing his heart out in front of me, saying, "Father, do understand! I'm not simply making all this up, that's the life we've actually led. We're never on our own—we can't even wash ourselves—three years like that!" And the mother was mad.

A few months ago I saw a big eighteen-year-old girl who had thrown herself in the Seine. We fished her out and asked her where she lived. And she took us to Ivry, and what we discovered was a hole in the ground, with no walls, nothing, a hole dug for the foundations of a house that had never been built. There, and they had been living in it for four months, were eleven people. It was closed up with bits of wood and rags, and as it had been raining for some time it had become a sort of swamp or cess-pit. And the girl had had enough of it: she had gone and thrown herself into the river. . . . All our friends were called together, and I told them about it, and we found a bit of land for them and worked night and day for seven days a week. With 150,000 francs worth of stuff, plaster, doors and windows we had salvaged, we built them a little house. The Sunday after it was finished we went to the mother and said simply, "It's for you." When she saw it she started to cry and we thought she was going to faint.

And there were similar cases every day.

There was that woman who came weeping to us because her husband had turned the gas on: he had decided to do away with them all because he knew that in a few days' time they were to be turned out. They had searched and searched, but in vain. So they had grown desperate. . . .

I think of the woman who had run away after she had been evicted, while her husband was looking for somewhere else to live. He was a clerk on the railway. We looked for this woman for twenty-four hours and found her the following night with her two children clutched to her. They hadn't slept or eaten anything all day. She was quite numb, and wet through from sitting in the grass at the side of the Marne. She had gone there to throw herself into the water with her children, but had not been able to make up her mind to do it and had simply stayed there, stupefied.

I think of that boy on Christmas Eve, three years ago. The day before, he had come into a little room we had built for him, the first room of a house that he is now in process of enlarging. He had three children and a fourth was on the way. When I arrived on Christmas Eve to give him my Christmas greetings, he looked at me and said, "Father, it must be true that there's a God and that he is good—you are a man of God and you have done this for me, got me a house. . . ." He went on, "Father, I have three young children, and there is going to be a fourth, and this evening I was just sitting here thinking"—the wife and children were in bed and asleep— "that this is the first time in my life that I have ever been able to be alone: the first time since I was married that I have been able to be alone, except during the summer when we could sleep out in the fields at night." That was the condition a French workman had been reduced to in that year of grace 1952! And how many more like him!

One day the priest in one of the neighbouring parishes called on me for help. "Father, come at once," he said; "they have just found a family in my parish living under a tarpaulin out in a field." I went to see them. The priest had not been able to find anyone to put them up. I found that they had been living there for eight months. The man worked in the local factory. When he got home from work he used to crawl under this tarpaulin on all fours to be with his wife and child. The child was a little boy and his wife was pregnant. When I looked up the family's record I found that there should have been three children, not one. A fourth was on the way. Two of the children had died: there was the baby there: the whole family was there under that tarpaulin, on the wet earth. . . .

It was then that I realised some terrible things.

OUR TREMENDOUS COWARDICE

I realised that so long as people who were supposed to be apostles, as long as a priest like me was incapable of saying to that poor woman, "Come on, get your things, pick up your child and come along with me and your husband and sleep in my room: I'll take your place in the tent and tomorrow we'll find some way of solving this"—until then, well, fundamentally I was simply a humbug.

In point of fact if I had talked to that poor woman, who had seen two of her children die, who was possibly expecting the one that was to be born to go the same way, and might even have been tempted to do away with it herself, if I had started talking to her about heaven and hell and the law of God, and told her that she had no right to do it, that it would be a crime—I was in process of discovering that if I told her all that and then, having had my little say, left her in her tent in her field, to her misery and distress, whilst I, the priest, went back to my room, a poor room, no doubt, but even so a real room, where I could put an electric fire on when it turned cold, and could sleep peacefully in my bed, and be alone—if, after my little sermon, I failed to take her to some more cheerful place than her own, well, then, she was bound to think to herself, "No doubt! It's all very fine what he says! Very true! But of course he's just a humbug like all the rest, for he's left me here in these dreadful conditions. . . ."

That's what I realised!

Oh, we all ought to come to realise that! So long as we are incapable of behaving like Our Lord, that is to say becoming incarnate, that is to say going down and sharing the pain and suffering of the people we are supposed to be leading into the way of truth—well, in point of fact we are simply humbugs.

ROOM FOR THE DEAD

A few months ago, for the first time, one of our fellow workers, a member of our Society of Ragpickers, died amongst

The first winter on the rubbish dumps was very tough.

No truck was too old to be persuaded to get moving.

"The real blasphemy is not the despairing curse of a man impotent to relieve his children's sufferings. It is the indifference of the well-to-do in face of the profanation of God's image in the destitute."

us. He was a Belgian who had once been in the Foreign Legion, a man who had suffered much. When we learned that there was no chance of his recovering we decided to go and fetch him from the hospital where he was being looked after and bring him back with us. For two whole weeks he was given as much care and attention as he would have got from his own family. Quite spontaneously our comrades stayed up in relays of two throughout the night to look after him. He died like a saint, offering up his life for Emmaus and his comrades.

When he died we had a meeting and decided that we wouldn't let him go to the common grave but would pool our bit of money as ragpickers, buy a plot of land in the cemetery and build our own communal vault, so that everyone would realise that our friendship went as far as that, into eternity. We went to the local office, where we were given a very friendly reception, and had all the rules explained about building our own vault. Now when we came out of the office the comrade who was with me said a terrible thing, an absolutely transfixing thing, one of those things that can only be said by the poor, because they see things that we have grown quite incapable of seeing. When we got out into the street all he said was, "Well, Father, after all that, with all these rules we've been told about for building the vault, Joseph will have more space now that he is dead than he had when he was alive." And it was true. It had never occurred to me to think of it like that.

If anybody tried to bury six adults and two young children within a space of about a hundred square feet, the size of the room at Montreuil, the law would forbid it: the police would come and dig the bodies up and then they would be buried again more appropriately. But when there are tens of thou-

sands of men and women, fathers and mothers, with feelings
just like yours and mine, and little children, living in agony,
dying, rebelling against it all, or, what is worse than rebellion,
growing brutish in such conditions, then we are quite indifferent and never lose a wink of sleep over it. We couldn't care
less! The police would be called in to dig up the dead bodies
and bury them differently, but no one thinks of coming to the
help of people actually living in such conditions.

DUTY OR KINDNESS

See here, my friends, you must understand this quite
clearly: when you are faced with a problem like this, it is not
true to say, as so many people do say, that it is a problem of
human kindness, a case of having pity, giving out of pity,
kindness, goodness of heart. It isn't true that a problem like
this, the problem of finding accommodation for working people so that they can have some sort of shelter for their wives
and children, it isn't true that this is a problem that involves
benevolence or being charitable or having a kind heart. Living
space for the working man is not a matter of kindness. We
really have to understand this. It is a question of justice,
something sacred, and we are simply behaving like cowards if
we try to turn it into a matter of kindness. We really have to
understand this. There will always be a need for human charity, there will always be a need for human kindness. In the
most perfectly just society in the world there will always be
something wrong, some snag, some unexpected reversal that
means that one has to come to the aid of one's friends. There
will always be moral difficulties, needing friendship. But in the
case of a problem like our present one, the first thing that is
needed is justice, not almsgiving.

Giving money for our schools, for charitable societies, for building a church and so on, is of course lawful and praiseworthy in the sight of God. But what is it all worth if we haven't already done all we can to give the workers their due, to give them the things they need and have not obtained? That, quite simply, is what the Gospel means.

We have to realise what our first duties are, the duties that come before all others.

We have all to realise this.

CHAMPS FLEURIS

Faced with all this suffering, it became necessary to do something about it.

When I found that family out in the fields I said to my companions, "Besides putting up these first five families we need to set about doing something to house the hundreds who keep coming and telling us how desperate they are."

I went back to the house. I said to them again, "This can't go on. We must do something, however poor we may be." We were living as ragpickers, of course, eighteen of us, all together. I said to them, "We must find some land and we must do some more building." So we started looking out for something. There was no road to the site we found, but we could see to that later, for a piece of land on a road would have been far beyond our means. It was an enormous piece of land, about eight thousand square yards. I was by this time no longer a deputy; I wouldn't join in with the new electoral system, and from the end of June I had had nothing in the way of money, nothing coming in at all. In my younger days I had been well off, but at the age of nineteen I had given all that up and I had never felt any desire for money since. When I gave up

being a deputy all I had was my huts and mattresses and these
few men on my hands. . . .

"Father, it's madness," they said. "You'll never be able to
pay." Whereupon I made another of my historic replies.
"How silly it is of you to say that!" I said. "When you've got
no money to pay with, that's just the time to take as much as
you can!"

And that's how we came to buy the land for our first estate.
I persuaded the owner to agree to being paid over a period of
ten years, at so much a month—he wasn't losing by it: it
meant that he got double the actual amount. And we at once
set about making a twenty-five-foot road; we made nineteen
gardens; we got the most down-and-out families together and
we set to work. I went to see second-hand dealers about stuff
taken from demolished property (of course I asked for credit),
and we started building the first house. At the way into the
field we put up a board, "Champs Fleuris, Campers' Association."

That was quite illegal, of course. We had no permit to do
so, there was no water, no electricity, the road was hardly
visible—so I said to my comrades, "We must work quickly so
that we can get a house finished and people in it before they
start taking proceedings against us, because once there is
somebody actually in there's a complicated procedure needed
to get the Prefect's signature authorising force to get them out.
And then it won't be such an easy matter getting them out
because they won't know where to put them and the authorities won't know what to do about it. So let's get on with it!"

We worked at top speed late into the night with the help
of truck headlamps, and before long the first house was finished, a very pretty little house it was too, with two rooms
made of double wooden walls. And when the new arrival,

Annie, came into the world, she was the first child to have
the Emmaus ragpickers to thank for being born with a roof
over her head.

And we got straight on with the job. We built three houses,
four, five. . . .

THE ARM OF THE LAW

Then one day the inevitable happened. Somebody came
along and asked to see my building permit.

Well, of course, we had never been able to ask for a building permit. What we were doing was quite illegal. So I said
to the official, "You are doing your job, sir, and you are quite
right, you will get a commendation. It is your duty to come
and try to catch me out, but I warn you that if you come
here again asking to see this building permit without also finding some means or other of enabling decent working families
to find the money for a bit of land with a road to it and some
means of getting a loan from the state, I shall put up a great
placard at the entrance to our Champs Fleuris estate. I shall
stick on it all the official particulars concerning the birth of
the men and women and children who have come to live here;
I shall get in touch with the newspapers, the radio, the cine-
mas, television, the lot—and over those official particulars,
with a bucket of whitewash and a brush I shall write 'LIV-
ING PERMIT'—for if we are not prepared to help these
people to get somewhere to live legally, we have no right to
refuse them any chance they may get, even if it is illegal."

I went on, "I prefer to see them living illegally rather than
dying legally like the children of that poor woman who has
had three children and now has only one. Yes, sir, 'LIVING

PERMIT'—because even in the case of people with no money there is a certain law that comes before all others, and that is their right to live like human beings." And the official went off.

A little later, someone came and threatened me with a legal action. "I beg and implore you," I said, "for the love of God, *do* bring an action against us. It's all we need. I want to have the chance of shouting the real truth about the situation in a court, face to face with the authorities. I shall put on all my decorations, my deputy's scarf, and my priest's stole on top of it all, if necessary, and go and tell that court the truth about this social order which we are supposed to be violating. It is an order which certainly has some good points, and we all benefit from it to some extent, but so long as it includes shameful and abominable things like this we shall be quite ready to violate it!

"So long as that woman was sleeping in a tent and watching her children die, everything was quite in order. The owner of the land had given permission to have the tent there, so that wasn't a crime. It was all quite regular. The children died quite legally. They were buried quite legally. I haven't a doubt of it. The mother might get tuberculosis, and she'd be sent quite legally to a sanatorium. The father might despair, and, as happens from time to time, throw himself under a train on the métro; they'd send him, quite legally, to the morgue. But if, one day, that man, who is a father as much as anyone else, as much as the policeman who comes to arrest him, by playing an accordion in a café at night gets enough bank notes to buy some corrugated iron and boards and tries—for the sake of the baby who's on the way—to build a little house: then, just because that man hasn't saved 350,000 francs (which is really the sum total of his crime), our social order regards what he is doing to save his child as a crime.

"So," I said, "I want to have the chance of shouting in court in the name of the Gospel that such a social order has got to be violated even to the end of the world, if necessary, so as to force it to correct itself, and change, and cease to be such a monstrosity, and so as to protest against such hypocrisy and to save the lives of our brothers."

AN ILLUSION

I don't want to cause anyone unnecessary pain, but I believe that there are certain truths which need to be said to those, in particular, who spend such a lot of money on covering our walls with posters (on the principle of replying to other posters)—to those who take refuge in fine words like "peace" and "freedom" and plaster the country with slogans of a more or less humorous and not always totally truthful character. I want to say to them, "But aren't you ever going to understand that a man who has to sleep out of doors at the end of a day's work isn't going to care about peace, freedom and justice if, for him, peace and justice mean sleeping out of doors? So long as you are unable to stick up posters saying, 'Here are the homes we have built and the people we have housed,' you are wasting your time on all this literature; for what people really want, first and foremost, is to know where they will get the most houses, where they can find the best chance for men, women and children *not* to die of exposure."

OUR FIRST LEGAL VICTORIES

No one brought an action against us. We went on building. And now, at last, victory began—on a very small scale. The

first sign was a Government circular regularising the position:
"We are aware of the illegality of the measures taken by Abbé
Pierre, but since he has promised to provide the requisite road
afterwards . . . since he has . . . given that . . . etc., etc. . . .
he is to be allowed to finish the work." I had said to the
minister, "I wonder just how you mean to go about stopping
us from finishing it—unless you provide houses for them yourself!" But the circular added, "If you hear of anything similar
being started elsewhere, you must let us know at once."

So, since we had nearly finished the nineteen houses of
Champs Fleuris, we said, "Thank you, monsieur le ministre,"
and started straight away on Les Coquelicots, a second estate
of fourteen new houses.

And there, two months later, we had our real victory.

Because we didn't give up, because we went on, we had our
first real victory: the Government's decision to authorise
advance loans from the family allowance funds for building
houses. This didn't solve everyone's problem, but it was the
beginning of a solution for a large number of families.

So, to prove that we weren't criminal types doing things
illegally out of sheer perversity, we started straight away on a
legal building-project with loans from the family allowance
people; our community worked on it voluntarily, half of them
doing ragpicking so as to keep the other half who did the
building.

We bought a new five-acre site on five years' credit: La
Pepinière at Pontault, Seine-et-Marne. We cleared it and
began laying on the amenities—roads, water, electricity. We
got together thirty-three families and began; this time we
asked for a permit to build our little houses, each at a cost of
about 1,800,000 to 2,000,000 francs,* with a loan from the

* Around $6,000.

building fund. These ones weren't just emergency huts; they were good, solid, detached houses. And some of our families who, three years earlier, would have had to provide three hundred and fifty thousand to start building could now begin to acquire possession of these houses for a mere initial payment of ten thousand francs. Now they have a home; they have twenty-five years in which to pay back the money borrowed; and they have the joy of being in their pretty little house.

After La Pepinière we went on to Torcy and Bouquet. We could soon count three hundred homes either finished or in construction.

DISTRESS VILLAGE

But all the time we were doing this, the more we built the more families came to ask for help. We got more and more desperate. As soon as we had a home for one family, ten more came. When we had housed the ten, a hundred more came. We couldn't cope. What could we do under such pressure— and some of these families were imploring us in utter despair, because they were living in impossible conditions.

We did a crazy thing. With some of our ragpicking money we bought a bit of the forest of Pomponne, fifteen miles from Paris. We made a clearing and put up tents, caravans and old vans. There were soon thirty families there who had been sleeping out of doors, a hundred children found lost in the forest, and families who could no longer afford 600 or 700 francs a night for a hotel room.

What a miserable solution it was! The men had to bicycle fifteen miles to work, or go three miles on foot to catch a train.

There was no water, nor electricity, nor drainage. Yet such were the conditions in which these families had been living that they thought such wretchedness as this less wretched than life as they had known it before.

One day a high official of the Department turned up. I happened to be there. He came up to me and said, "This is an atrocious state of affairs! We can't have people living like this in 1953! There's no sanitation. How dare you? etc., etc." I got angry in the end. "Monsieur le Directeur," I said, "I rather think you've come to the wrong address. *You* come and tell *me* these things! As if these people were *my* job! I gather you're in charge of sanitation; well, provide sanitation for them—it's your job, not mine! What's stopping you from giving them sanitation? If all you want is the owner's permission, it's yours here and now. *You* come and tell *me* that there's no sanitation? That was a mistake, as you know very well; some of these families were living sixty to a basement, with one lavatory. What we have here is hygiene—they've got the whole forest! There are a hundred thousand people in the slums for whom *you* are responsible who have less sanitation than we have here, and you never do anything active or practical for them. They are better off here, both from the point of view of human dignity and of health. You only have to look at the kids' faces; the moment there's a gleam of sun they rush off to play in the wood. Where they were before there wasn't any sun, and as soon as it rained the area turned into a sewer. Take those ones. There were seventeen of them living in two small rooms. Here, each household is private. At least they have the minimum dignity which makes human life worthy of the name. You know very well that they are really less badly off here. Anyway, the proof of it is that they prefer to stay. They came of their own free will, and there are no cops at the gate to stop them going away. They came because they are less badly off here than where they were before. As for you, you clever man, tell me where we ought to put them. We have some trucks, and I can telephone my friends; they can be here within an hour, and they can take these families anywhere you say."

He had nothing to say. He went.

DON'T LOOK

Then I said to myself, "This may be bad for my record." When I got home I telephoned the Prefect. He wasn't there, and I spoke to the official in charge of his office. We had a good argument and finished up as friends, because he was a good man and he understood.

I said: "I want to report that there has been an incident: rudeness to an important official. But you must let me explain. When you come and accuse me of keeping those families in bad housing conditions, you really know quite well that it's a farce. You know very well that it isn't the bad conditions that you mind, because you know that they are less badly off there than where they were before. The real accusation, the thing you can't forgive me, is that I've taken them out of the dark cellars and fantastic slums where they used to be, where they were distributed and hidden and invisible. What you can't forgive me is having gathered them together and put them out in the sun, in public, and thrown them and their wretchedness in society's teeth. It's *that* that interferes with your digestion and your sleep!"

And that's the truth.

Everyone of us, myself included, is a bit of a hypocrite. As soon as wretchedness disappears from sight we quickly manage to become indifferent to it. We are much more concerned to have it hidden than to have it eradicated. As long as wretchedness doesn't show itself, as long as it has the good taste to refrain from spoiling our happiness and our little bit of comfort and security, as long as we can't *see* it, we are content.

Perhaps the most important thing we have done is to have had the courage to be uncivilised, to do what "isn't done," to say the things that mustn't be said; to challenge the unconscious hypocrisy of happy people, throwing in their teeth the unpleasant sight of the suffering and unjust distress of unhappy people, after coming face to face with it ourselves and plunging right into the middle of it.

This surely must be the first job to be done, and our first duty.

THE EMERGENCY HOUSING AMENDMENT

It was then that, with some friends, we worked out a legal measure which I wanted to have voted in Parliament as part of the Budget—the "Emergency Housing" plan which has since become famous. It was a very modest plan. We only asked for one thousand million francs out of the ninety thousand million allocated in the Budget to cheap housing; one thousand million to be devoted to a special, top-priority programme of building, to put up tenements quickly which could be finished in detail later on, and which, meanwhile, would mean that the largest possible number of basic dwellings would be produced.

We were only asking for one thousand million for these emergency blocks. We wanted to be able to provide something better than camps of tents and trucks. We just wanted one thousand million, so that we could start building, and show what could be done in the way of homes costing about eight hundred thousand francs.

It was not a question of temporary buildings or barracks. These blocks are built in parpen or brick, capable of lasting a hundred years; they consist of apartments to meet the most urgent needs of all, apartments with a floor-space of about forty square yards—one good room, two little bedrooms, a kitchen, shower, toilet, and a bit of garden. All this for a rent of three thousand francs a month—less, with the rent allowance.

These flats were planned to correspond precisely to the needs of two categories of people. First, young couples. During the first four or five years of marriage, when the children are small, they need no more than this. They only ask, instead of spending all their money on slum-dwellings or hotel rooms, to have somewhere with the essential modern conveniences—hot water and electricity—so that during these four, five or six first years, while they rent a little place of this sort, they can prepare for the future, save up, and so get ready to make themselves a larger, permanent home later on.

But they are not needed only for young couples. They are wanted for another category of people too—the elderly couples who hang on obstinately to a home which has grown far too big for them after their children have married. It is easy enough to understand. These old folk are afraid. They don't know what is to become of them if they go, so they won't give in. But if we could assure these elderly couples that they could have a nice little place in a suburb somewhere, a ground-floor apartment with all modern conveniences at a low rent, it would be paradise for them, and far more comfortable than anything they had in their old home.

These apartments would be a good start for young couples and a haven for the old.

I dream of the day when we shall see all our towns building blocks of this sort in sufficient quantities to meet the needs of all the young couples and old people. I often say that we shall not be truly civilised until the day comes when, to each boy and girl coming before him to be married, the mayor can hand, in the name of the commune, not only their family allowance book but a rent book entitling them to five or six years in a "good start house."

When that day comes, we shall have saved the future of France. We shall have restored the gift of hope to all the young people who are now drifting in a state of despair, ruining the lovely freshness of their first years of love in terror of having a child because they'll be turned out of their hotel room and won't know where to go; the young people who are ruining the best years of their lives, losing their health and breaking their hearts, demoralised by living in impossible conditions and not knowing what is to become of them tomorrow.

We shall save the youth of France the day when we can carry out this programme of emergency housing, which will give us time to go on to the other kinds of housing which are also necessary.

That was the request we made.

DEATH OF A BABY

Well, you know what happened.

The debate at the Palais Bourbon was on the night of the 3rd of January. The session had already gone on and on interminably. When our proposal came up for debate everyone was tired, with no idea except to go home and be warm and sleep. So they polished off the question in a hurry; people were heard to say that it was a crazy idea, plans of this sort were quite superfluous, in three years' time there would be too many houses. Our plan was turned down.

Now it was on that very night, the 3rd of January, that the temperature suddenly went down to minus ten degrees centigrade.

Next day, very early in the morning, just as I flung myself on the daily papers to see how the debate had gone and whether we had got what we asked, there was a knock at the door. It was one of my friends, white-faced, who said, "Father, the baby died last night." It was one of the families that we were building for. The cold had held up the work, and they were still living in a derelict car, at Les Coquelicots, beside their unfinished house. And during the night the baby had died.

Perhaps the two had to come together—the rejection of our request to Parliament and the death of my friend's child, to have the effect on me which they did.

Next night I couldn't sleep in the room where I live. There is nothing luxurious about it, but I was ashamed to think of all the families with even less. I walked up and down and round and round. It was then, between midnight and five in the morning, that I wrote to the Minister of Reconstruction.

Whenever I tell this story, I want to make a point of stressing how much respect we owe that man, though his opinions on many matters certainly do not coincide with mine.

I wrote simply, without weighing my words, just as they came, and after I had told him the story I finished my letter by saying: "Monsieur le Ministre, the day after tomorrow at

two o'clock in the afternoon we shall bury the baby who died
of cold while the National Assembly was rejecting the emergency building plan. It would be a good thing if you were with
us. They are not wicked people. They will not give you a bad
reception, and it will restore their hopes, because they will
say, 'If he is a man at all, it's not possible that after seeing
this he won't change and do something real for us.' "

THE STATE SPEAKS

You know what happened then. At the last moment, a
quarter of an hour before the funeral, the telephone rang:
"The Minister has just decided that someone else can go to
the opening of the new houses at Choisy-le-Roi, and he will
come to the funeral of the baby who died at Les Coquelicots."

I was overwhelmed. I went down there and it happened,
as a strange coincidence, that our two cars met head-on in a
traffic block in a narrow street. He had to reverse. We went
on in that order to the crossroads. When we both got out I
was crying. I was simply overwhelmed. I just said, "It's here.
Come."

I think it must be long since any such sight was seen anywhere in the world. There was this man, a Cabinet Minister,
bareheaded, with his car with its cockades coming along far
behind, walking for about a mile in the cold behind a pau-
pers' hearse bearing the coffin of a working-class child who
had died of poverty. He walked bareheaded, this Cabinet
Minister, all alone in the middle of twenty rough, uncouth
men, of whom more than one had tried conclusions before
now with the forces of law and order. . . . That cortège of

twenty down-and-outs suddenly put on a level with the Minister following that little child's coffin was something overwhelming. It was said afterwards, "It was a national funeral, a funeral of national shame"—a hard saying, but true.

When we came out of the church the Minister said to me, "I've come, as you see. I admit that I have never seen such poverty before, but I am not incapable of understanding." I said, "Monsieur le Ministre, we appreciate your gesture and we thank you, but what will count with us is not that you came but what you are going to do now." Then he said, "Give me your telephone number; we must meet again."

I had to go away that very evening to the mountain in the Aveyron where we were demolishing shanties. We had a whole team of ragpickers there. I told him that I should be back two days later. He telephoned as soon as I was back. We spent a whole morning splashing round the building sites, and at the end of that morning he announced that the emergency building plan which had been turned down a few days earlier would be put into action after all.

And today, thanks to the whole of France, that plan has been launched.

DYING IN THE STREETS

The weeks went by. It was nearly the end of January, and the cold got steadily worse.

Every evening when I came back to Paris with the trucks after doing a day's ragpicking I saw more and more men on the pavements near the Gare de Lyon and the Gare d'Austerlitz, crouching over the warm ventilators. You could see them in the centre of the town in front of the ventilators of the shops, at ten or eleven o'clock at night, trying to get a little warmth from the central heating system inside.

One night I could stand it no longer. I stopped to talk to the poor souls. We gave them what we had. When I came back home I said to the others, "Here is something else that can't go on. We must put on some sort of night-service. We'll empty a truck each evening, have a quick supper, load it up again with bread, wine, soup and blankets, and go out into the night to do what no one else is bothering to do. We'll take them *some* help, anyway."

We began. Every night up to two or three o'clock in the morning we went through the streets, and every night we found a larger number of people in this desperate condition. There were more every night because the colder it got, the more people there were who would normally have taken shelter in cellars, garrets and sheds, with no heating and the wind blowing through the walls, and who now, feeling the chill of death on them, got up to tramp the streets rather than die where they lay.

IF YOU CAN DO IT FOR DOGS . . .

Next day I was due to broadcast on television on a completely different subject. It was on direct transmission, with no censorship. Suddenly, I couldn't hold out any longer. I was exhausted with fatigue and obsessed by what we saw every night, and in the end I dropped the subject I was supposed to be talking about. I described what we were doing every night, and I cried out there in front of the television camera, "But after all, monsieur le Président of the Municipal Council of Paris, you have pounds for stray dogs; can't you do as much for the men who are dying on our pavements?"

One night we were doing our dreadful round looking for the people who sleep in the streets—who die in the streets, that is—and a friend was with us who had brought his car to help because one of the trucks had broken down. We got to one dark street and I said, "Stop, look down there." He said "What at? That's nothing, it's a pile of rubbish." I insisted, "No, I'm sure, come and see." The pile of rubbish consisted of two old men, blind. The temperature was ten degrees below freezing. They had crouched down on the pavement, their white sticks on the ground beside them; they were covered with sacks and rags. They were almost dying.

I've seen what it means to be a man crouching down to die in the middle of our civilised society. When a man stands upright he seems something immense, expansive, a figure that fills the sky; when he lies down on the ground to suffer and die he seems to become something invisible and insignificant and ridiculous. But that seemingly ridiculous something will rise up again one day, the Day of the Lord, and will stand for our overwhelming and our condemnation. It is so.

FORBIDDEN WORDS

When we went about like this at night we discovered something else—a frightful discovery. These people who were in such distress, the ones to whom we took food and covering on those first nights when we did not know of any shelter where we could take them—we realised that their situation was so

horrible and hopeless that it was, so to speak, impossible to
say anything to them—to say those simple, elementary things
which pass between man and man the world over excepting
only between mortal enemies. When the time came to leave
them, after giving them something to eat, these ordinary,
simple words seemed to freeze on our lips. One night I was
on the point of saying "Good night" to one of them, as anyone does to anyone else, and I suddenly realised how gro-
tesque it was. Those simple words had become monstrous.
Good night! The very speaking of the words was forbidden,
they were so absurd. And so I and the friend who went with
me used to flee away like thieves and malefactors without
saying anything at all. There was nothing we could say to
them. We would think how, that night, when we had finished,
when we had given away everything we had with us, we
should be going back to a *house*, to a bit of shelter, where
we could go to bed in the warmth, while we left them on
the pavement.

It was like that every night. And every night we came
home more ashamed.

RUE DE LA MONTAGNE-SAINTE-GENEVIEVE

And then one day—it was a Friday, at eleven o'clock in
the morning, when I was saying Mass, after getting back
very late and being caught at once by the post and a pile of
things to do, and managing at last to escape to the chapel—
an idea came to me which was to be the beginning of great
things. I suddenly remembered that a few days earlier a man
had written to me saying, "Father, I have a piece of land.

It is in the Rue de la Montagne-Sainte-Geneviève. There was a house on it which has been demolished, but I haven't the money to rebuild. So, if it is of any use to you, the site is at your disposal." I had filed the letter, not having the least idea of anything we could do with it. We hadn't the money any more than he. And what use was a bare site?

And now, suddenly, the idea came. I remembered that we had a Jewish friend at Montreuil who sold Government surplus. We had often bought tents from him for our families. I knew he had some very big ones. I said to myself, "That would be the very thing! I must ask him to give us one of those tents, and we'll pitch it there." As soon as I came out of the chapel I rushed to the telephone and rang his number. "Listen. You're a Jew and I'm a priest, but there are men and women in our streets, brothers and sisters of ours, who are dying of poverty. Wouldn't it be grand if you came along this evening to a site that someone has offered us, with your workmen and one of your tents, while we come with our rag-pickers? We'll put up that tent in the very middle of Paris, we'll put straw inside, and heaters, and we'll buy a battery for light and put in a lavatory at the back, and then, at night, instead of just giving these people who are suffering so much a bit of bread, we can say, 'Come along, there's a place here where you can be warm.'" He said, "Good enough. I'll be there this evening."

And that Friday evening he was there and we pitched the tent. By ten o'clock we had put down a ton of straw, and we went off rejoicing in the thought that we should be able to take some of them, at least, out of the cold.

From that very first evening the tent was too small. There were sixty of them in it already!

Next day was Saturday, and then Sunday the 31st of January.

COURBEVOIE: THE FIRST COMMITTEE FOR AID TO THE HOMELESS

I had a longstanding promise to go and talk that day in the church at Courbevoie. It is a working-class parish. I preached there all that Sunday morning.

Between two of the Masses I was called to the telephone in the sacristy. It was a friend of mine who had spent all the previous night, Saturday and Sunday, going with us to take food to the unfortunates in the streets. When we had left to go to bed he had gone on alone. He arrived at the Boulevard Sébastopol just at the moment when they were picking up a poor woman who was dying; she died as they got to the police station. All they found on her was a piece of paper; the eviction order which had been served on her in the name of the law—the law which exists for the protection of us privileged people—to turn her out of her attic, two days earlier, because she owed 8,000 francs in rent. She died on the pavement, in the middle of Paris, at three o'clock in the morning. My friend had telephoned to tell me about it; I told the story in the remainder of my sermons. People didn't want to believe that it was true!

On that one morning of the last day of January—before the things began happening which made us really famous—the parishioners of Courbevoie gave us 750,000 francs to help homeless people. They came to me after the last Mass saying, "Father, we must go to the *mairie* this evening and tell the whole population what you told us in your sermon."

The meeting was rapidly organised. I cried out that evening: "We've got beyond emergency building, you see. . . . What we have to organise is in the nature of first-aid! . . . With children dying of cold within a few yards of us, there's only one legitimate attitude for all decent people, no matter which side they are on politically: the will in each person to co-operate to the full, so far as in him lies, to bring this state of affairs to an end."

They decided on the spot to form a committee. It was the first committee for emergency aid to the homeless. The committee included the priest, the anti-clericals, the M.R.P. (Christian Democrats), the R.P.F. (Gaullists), and militant Communists. Everyone who was there, in fact. And there and then they decided to open two centres. They furnished them with heaters, straw mattresses, and blankets, and they went out that night to fetch in the unfortunate men, women and children who, as I had told them, were sleeping out in the streets in larger numbers every night.

Being very tired, I went to sleep at a friend's house in Courbevoie. I was all in. For the last fortnight I had been spending every night, up to three in the morning, with my ragpicking friends, collecting people, feeding them and giving them clothes.

THE MORNING OF THE 1ST OF FEBRUARY 1954

But they came to wake me in the morning. They were all there, and they said to me, "Father, when we went off yesterday evening we were saying to each other, 'Abbé Pierre is right; these unfortunate people exist and we must go and help them.' But when we came back we were horror-struck. After

driving the trucks round up to three in the morning, we
realised that of the hundred and twenty or hundred and
thirty men and women we had collected, eighty per cent
weren't tramps or drunks or professional vagabonds at all.
They were ordinary men and women. Eighty per cent of them
were under forty years old, half of them under thirty. There
were men who wept and said, 'Give us work, and rooms that
we can pay for by working!' There were men who worked all
day in a factory and, because they had no lodgings, had
dumped their wife and children with a friend. And because
the friend hadn't room for everyone, they would leave the
factory in the evening and go and have a bite with the kids
and the wife and then—go away again: leave them, as soon
as night had really come, to walk the streets and stamp their
feet on a warm ventilator, spend the whole night like that and
go off again in the morning to the factory."

So all these friends at Courbevoie besought me, "Father,
we can never manage alone. We must talk to the Radio
people. You must tell everyone what you have made us
realise."

So we threw a few sentences together and I telephoned the
Radio. At first the director said, "You're crazy! The Radio
doesn't belong to me, it's a public service—I should have to
ask for official authorisation. I can't change the whole programme like that, five minutes before it's published for the
day." Then the friend who was with me and was listening
took the receiver and said, "You're quite right, sir, it's true.
Speaking administratively, and as an official, you have no
right to accept our request. But have you thought of this: if
you refuse, it is possible that tomorrow morning, when you
open your paper, you will have to consider that it is your fault

that someone—reported as having been picked up dead of cold and hunger—has died in that desperate state because *you* refused to broadcast this appeal?" There was a few seconds' silence, and then the man said briskly, "You're right. Dictate your appeal, and I'll pass it on to the Radio."

I know that he came in for a severe censure that evening and next day. But I also know that two days later he was a great man, because it was the whole people of France who declared him justified in having managed that day to forget his administrative position and act, however irregularly, in favour of the children and the people who were suffering.

He was right! And it was because of him that the whole thing got under way.

THE APPEAL

A quarter of an hour later I was rushing off to Radio Luxemburg to broadcast the appeal myself:

"My friends, this is a call for help. A woman has just died, frozen to death, at three o'clock last night on the pavement of the Boulevard Sébastopol, clasping in her hand the paper which had given the order to evict her the day before yesterday.

"Every night more than two thousand people crouch down in the street, in the frost, without a roof over their heads or bread to eat. Many of them are half naked.

"Listen. To meet a horror like this even the priority building programme isn't priority enough.

"Within three hours, two emergency centres have come into existence, one in a tent in the Rue de la Montagne-Sainte-

Geneviève, the other at Courbevoie. They are overflowing already. They need to be opened everywhere.

"What is needed is that this very night, in every town in France and every district of Paris, posters shall go up, with a light to shine on them at night, at the doors of places where there will be blankets, straw and soup: posters headed 'Fraternal Emergency Centre,' followed by these simple words:

> " 'Whoever you are, if you are suffering,
> Come in, sleep, eat and take heart.
> This is where you are loved.'

"The meteorological office tells us to expect a month of terrible frost. As long as the winter lasts these centres must stay.

"Faced with their brothers dying of poverty, men should have only one opinion: the will to stop it from going on any longer.

"I beg and beseech you! Let us have enough love here and now to do this much! Let it be seen that so much suffering has at least given us back one wonderful thing: the soul of France.

"Thank you!"

I had added, "Bring your gifts and your help to the Hôtel Rochester, 92, Rue de la Boétie."

Why the Hôtel Rochester? It is a luxury hotel just off the Champs-Elysées, and not a place that I knew. I had never been there, I didn't know the proprietor; and yet, on the spur of the moment, I said on the Radio, "Bring whatever you want to bring there." I knew it was a place I could count on. Why? Quite simply, because the proprietor had written to me a week before. And what that generous-hearted woman had said was simply this: "Father, since hearing that there are babies dying of cold in Paris I can't sleep in peace at night, thinking how my hotel, at this time of year, always has empty rooms in it every night, and heated rooms at that. So I am putting twelve rooms in my luxury hotel at the disposal of any working-class families who don't know where to sleep tonight with their children. You can send them. My hotel is open to them." I had sent the first families along without having had any time to go myself. So that was how I knew I could trust her.

THE EXPLOSION

And the balloon went up!

The appeal went out at one-five or one-ten on the national Radio, at one-fifteen on Radio Luxemburg. When I arrived at the Hôtel Rochester at one-thirty there was already more than a cubic yard of blankets and clothes in the hall of the hotel. There was already a lot of money and jewellery deposited at the cash-desk. In all the streets radiating out from the Place de Saint-Philippe-du-Roule there were positive processions of thousands of people who had heard those few sentences on the Radio and snatched a coat from the press or a blanket from the bed and rushed out of their houses to hand in their bundles and bring their money! It is impossible to describe it. At the end of an hour they were having to divert the buses; it was impossible to move in the Rue La Boétie; they had to send extra police, and about five o'clock that afternoon it became urgently necessary to put in five, and soon afterwards it became eleven, extra telephone lines into the hotel.

We saw the most unheard-of sights. We saw a man arrive,

put down his bundle, go out into the street and then—the temperature was ten to twelve degrees below freezing—come back, take off his coat, throw it on the pile and go. Someone said to him, "You'll catch cold," and he said, "There are others who need it more than I do."

There were children who broke open their banks and gave everything they had.

There were old people who gave their rings, like one woman who wrote: "Father,"—she was an old lady—"I am very badly off. After listening to you I searched and I haven't anything to give; I only have just enough to live on. But while I was thinking my eye fell on my ring, and I said to myself, 'Now I'm an old woman, what good is it to me? If it could make it possible for the Father to put some mother into her own home one day sooner, I haven't any right to keep my ring.' " So she sent the one thing of value which she had, her wedding ring.

There were old men who sent me letters with ten fifteen-franc stamps in them. And there was a group of dustmen, men who collect the garbage in the streets of Paris, trade-unionists of the extreme left, people who vote Communist and not of my way of thinking at all, who came along and brought me a collection they had taken up amongst themselves to help us.

And I saw anonymous, unknown people that day; I shall never know who they were. One of them waited over an hour so as to give me his bundle himself; when his turn came to see me, he held out a little packet wrapped in newspaper. It looked like a book. I said, "What is it?" and asked him his name. He wouldn't answer, and went away. Late that evening —that night, in fact—I tidied up my papers and opened the packet. Inside that newspaper—and this happened twice—I found one million francs in ten-thousand-franc notes. Perhaps, for him—I know nothing about it—the million he gave was no more, and may have been less, than the ten fifteen-franc stamps sent by an old man in poor circumstances; perhaps that million wouldn't deprive him of one day's holiday or of butter on his table; I don't know. Again, perhaps it may have been an immense sacrifice. What is certain is that the anonymous people who did this thing did it with all their hearts.

And the post kept coming in with cheques and banknotes, until in a few weeks we had had three hundred thousand letters.

On the fifth day, the Saturday, when the bank where we had opened an account, so as to make everything public and open to investigation, telephoned to give me a statement, I was told that a hundred and fifty million francs had come in. In five days! By the eleventh day there two hundred and fifty million, given by the people of France.

NO HEARTLESS PEOPLE

I was told by the appropriate department of the Finance Ministry that, working out the sum total of what was given throughout France after that appeal on the 1st of February, by all sorts of people in all sorts of ways to all sorts of organisations engaged either in building or in sheltering people who had nowhere to go, that sum total, issuing spontaneously from the generosity of the people of France in response to an appeal on the 1st of February by an unknown voice, would amount to more than a thousand million francs. The people who were said to be degenerate, who were so spiritless, who could feel no enthusiasm for any great enterprise, who believed in nothing, who had confidence in nothing—some folk of whom they know nothing appeal to them, and they not merely *lend* but *give* a hundred and fifty million francs in five days. In a month and a half about five hundred million had come in.

That people suddenly proved itself capable of acting on such a scale as this—of doing something which went on, unflaggingly, week after week, turning the whole country upside down and even producing reactions far beyond our frontiers.

SEVENTY DAYS—FORTY-EIGHT HOMES

We went straight to work. I summoned the builders on that Saturday, the 5th of February, and said to them: "We have a site at Plessis-Trévise, which we bought a short while before all this happened but weren't able to pay for, though we began clearing it after making the first payment; start work there on Monday, beginning with the building of forty-eight houses." They answered, "What are we going to be paid with? It will take at least two or three months for the building fund to examine your references before they'll give you a loan. We can't work for two or three months without payment." I said to them, "Rest assured, you'll be paid. It's true that the building fund want several months, but, for once, it can take its time; this time the ragpickers will be lending to the building fund. It can repay as convenient." The work began.

Seventy days later we had finished clearing the ground, making the roads, and building forty-eight houses. Forty-eight families housed in seventy days! We started on the rest.

We were actually able to start immediately on fifteen hundred homes round Paris, not counting all the ones started by other organisations, with the help of the donations which came in and of the financial contribution made by the Government: they started a loan, which was not very brilliantly handled; in fact it got to the point where I had to wash my hands of it entirely, because the people who control the really large concentrations of capital wouldn't subscribe to it. The scandal was so great that at last I had to denounce it. All it was doing was taking subscriptions from small people while the big industrial powers and financiers turned up their noses at the loan because there was no interest involved in it. As though the only interest in life were money! As though children's lives were not more important than interest on investments!

The whole thing is now under way. We estimate that this year (1954) the number of homes built before the end of December will be almost double what it would have been if the storm had not broken as it did.

I recently read a report which showed that under the pressure of these events the average cost of building a house has come down by twenty-five per cent, because a tendency has set in which is the opposite of what had previously dominated the production of materials, plans and models. People have begun to understand that the time has passed when the most profitable thing to do was to build luxury apartments, which are now so numerous that there is no one to take them; they have realised that it is time at last, if only out of self-interest, to start building for more unfortunate, small people. The movement has started now, and it is nowhere near stopping.

Letters go on pouring in every day.

We poor ragpickers are budgeting for nearly two thousand million francs, including loans from the building fund, up to the end of December this year. We, on our own, have received more than five hundred million, and we have compelled the State to release credits to match for all the sites where we have begun work.

We are going on with the fight.

ACTION

Since then we have been campaigning throughout France for the creation of committees for organising building-sites— all kinds of ordinary building-sites and emergency housing sites, but also sites for camps like the one at Noisy-le-Grand. This is so as to be able to give shelter straight away, in tents or little huts like the ones we are beginning on now, at 250,000 francs apiece, made of fibro-cement, to the families in the streets. They are simply shelters, of two or three rooms each, where families can be temporarily housed—a big room in which the parents can sleep, and one bedroom for the boys and one for the girls.

We must have more and more of these in every town in France, even in the smaller towns where the problem may be less acute but where it does exist.

We must be in a position to face the population with this challenge. We need young families who, for the sake of being free and on their own, and no longer living as one of several households all on top of each other, have the courage to go and live in these camps. We need sites where we can put a drinking fountain and lay on electricity and where we can put more and more of these little houses, so as to make sure that members of local governments and people elected to the

In two years, nearly two thousand dwellings built, more than a million man-days of labour. The ragpickers cannot solve France's housing problem, but they make the shame of it public, intolerable. . . .

Tent dwellings at Vanves, at the Pont Sully, the Pont Tolbiac, against a background of luxury apartments (empty, often enough).

National Assembly and ministers of the Government can't shut their eyes to poverty because it is hidden. We must show it to them in public. All those who are too badly off in the conditions in which they now are must have the chance of living in shelters of this sort so that they can be free, with the dignity of a home of their own, and can know at the same time that, thanks to living like this, they are arousing public opinion and those in authority, and that this will help to bring victory at last and save everyone else too, because the necessary credits will be voted in the next budget and real building can begin.

THE FLEA

One day early in February, when the crowds were thronging the streets round the Hôtel Rochester, someone came to tell me that a Cabinet Minister had, in his innocence, wasted a quarter of an hour of a government council meeting drawing attention to the precautions that ought to be taken, since it was impossible to know what use that little priest might make of the extraordinary popularity which had descended on him, and the result might be a menace to public order!

When I heard this I telephoned the Prefect of Police, because I knew they were having a meeting there just then. I said, "I know you are having a meeting. If you don't mind, I'll come." I went. The meeting consisted of the President of the Municipal Council of Paris, the Prefect of the Seine, and the Prefect of Police. When they had finished their business I said, "Listen. I've come because there's something I must make clear to you. It appears that people are worried about the ambitions that I and my comrades may possibly have. So

I have come straight here to tell you that you are right, and you had better be very worried indeed, because we have perfectly terrible ambitions. The ambition we have, we ragpickers, is to be a flea hopping out of a ragpicker's dustbin right onto the Minister's desk, and biting him and shouting, 'Do your job! Wake up!' That's our ambition. And whoever may be in power, we mean to go on with it. We have made up our minds to be that flea, and to go on biting them, so as to remind them of the wretchedness of the people who are suffering and needing to be rescued."

POLITICAL INCONSISTENCY

One of the discoveries I have made, the lessons I have learnt, since living amongst those who suffer is a great principle of political philosophy. It applies to everyone, from the extreme left to the extreme right. I have discovered that the only basis for political understanding, meaning a practical understanding of problems according to their urgency, understanding of what needs to be done for the good of the community, is to share in a genuine and real way in the sufferings of those who suffer most within the community which one is supposed to be governing. I have discovered that men may come out top at college and be the most intelligent people on earth, but as soon as they start living in security, lacking nothing in a world where the majority lack even necessities, lacking nothing amidst people who lack everything, they go to pieces from the point of view of political understanding. They refuse to understand the real problems and real needs; they waste their time and energy on a mass of questions which may be very delicate and subtle but are quite secondary; they don't see that the primary problem is to build houses to put people in and schools where children can learn to read.

This year, more than ten thousand children in the Paris area were sent home—though the law demands that their parents send them to school—because we haven't been able to build enough schools for the children of France. How long are we going to go on with anomalies of this sort?

We can't build the houses and schools we need; we can't build the hospitals we need: we see people with tuberculosis dragging on in slums for six months on end, spitting out bacilli over their children, because there is no place for them in a sanatorium. We can't run to things like that, and then we waste time on a whole lot of luxury building in Paris! We don't know what to do with all the luxury apartments at twenty, twenty-five or thirty thousand francs a month; there are too many of them. Of course we know that we have to have some of them; a great country will always have to have some of them, but we say that it is a crime to have sunk so much of France's capital in financing these luxury buildings. There are so many of them that there aren't enough people to rent them, and work on them has stopped because the owners see that there are too many of them and they won't pay any more. So they stop work. And meanwhile we can't afford to build the simple apartments needed by the workers who, just as much as these others and indeed more than they, constitute the wealth of France.

We *must* protest, we *must* get this state of affairs reversed. I do not know who is going to be the next Minister. I do know that it depends on us to see that whoever the Minister is he does what is needed to ensure that *not one single stroke of work shall be done on luxury housing until we have all the housing we need at popular prices.*

THE TRUE GREATNESS OF A CITY

In any city, if it is to be a truly honourable city, the municipal council ought to be able to call a meeting of all the best architects in the district and say to them: "Draw up plans for the improvement of the city. Draw up some wonderful plans, so that our city will be the most beautiful city in the world." Then, later on, I should like to see the mayor call in the best painter in the district and say to him: "Paint us a wonderful mural in the middle of the town representing all the improvements the architects are planning." So I should like to see this mural set up at the town centre, in the public square, and have the mayor summon the whole population, with the fire-brigade and the band, to the unveiling of the mural; and I would have his whole speech on this occasion to consist of one paragraph written up over the mural, in which my intelligent and courageous mayor would say: "I hereby promise that I and the municipal council will gradually carry out these improvements to the town starting from the day when there is no longer one single homeless person in the town. I promise that until that day we shall not spend a penny on anything except building as many houses at popular prices as are needed."

Because it is a crime to spend vast sums of money on improvements which only serve the vanity of people who are well off and living in good houses, while there are masses of people still living in lodgings which are turning into slums because three families are living where only one should be.

We must go on shouting it over and over again. We must write it on all the walls and all the public monuments of our towns: The beauty of a town and the beauty of a nation does not lie in museums and theatres and public gardens, nor even in cathedrals. The beauty of a town, in the sight of God and of men, lies in not having slums and homeless people. That is the beauty of a town.

We have got to understand this, and to make up our minds to go on fighting until we have won. This is the battle which my comrades and I began fighting in the winter of 1954.

IT IS OURSELVES WE SHOULD ABUSE

When people cheer me as I go past, I always say to the ones who are cheering: "I haven't any illusions. You cheer me for two reasons. There are two elements in your cheering. One comes from the fact that you are all good-hearted souls; so you are glad to see someone looking after unfortunate people. That's a good thing, and you're quite right; but, goodness me, I'm not so simple as to think that that's all! There's another side to your cheering, which comes quite simply from the fact that you are good citizens like anyone else, and you rather like to hear someone tearing a strip off the authorities."

It's true, indeed it is! Don't deny it! We are all a bit like that, and I'm not reproaching you for it; after all, abusing the authorities a little does you good, and it won't do them any harm. So don't worry! But—attention, please! If we are to be perfectly clear and honest with ourselves, I think we need to add something further. If you like abusing the authorities and it does them a bit of good, too, that's fine; *but*—let's have the courage to take a look at ourselves. After heaping abuse on the authorities, let's keep some for ourselves; for what, in fact, do the events of last winter prove?

On the 3rd of January our Parliament and Government decided that the emergency building plan was a ridiculous daydream and turned it down. One month later, on the 4th of February, the same Parliament and the same Government —for once, miraculously, it hadn't changed in the meanwhile —the very same men decided that it was a matter of the most urgent urgency and that there was nothing that needed to be done quicker than these emergency buildings.

What had happened in that month to make the very same men decide that a thing was absolutely necessary which, a month earlier, they had said was idiotic? What had happened was quite simple. What had happened was that we had woken up; an appeal by a few poor devils of ragpickers had made us understand the problem, and we had risen up as one united nation and brought down our fist on the table shouting "We want emergency housing for the people who are worst off!" And, because we got to the point of demanding it as an obvious, indisputable thing, those who are in command had given way and obeyed us.

That, after all, as I was saying just now, is real democracy: being ourselves the ones who are suffering from these simple problems, so that we can be the first to say, "*This* is what is urgent. *We* know that this is what has to be done straight away."

The lesson we ought to have learnt from these events is that it was really we who were guilty, because all that was necessary was that we should manage to unite and shout aloud with one voice that we wanted this sane and simple thing! Since that was all that was needed to get things started, it proves that we are the guilty ones, for not having shouted sooner—you and I alike; for if we had shouted for it earlier we would have got it earlier. And this means that now we mustn't stop.

WORSE THAN REBELLION

When I talk in comfortable, well-housed circles it sometimes happens that people say to me, "Monsieur l'Abbé, if there were really such terrible distress as you say amongst the homeless people, there'd be a rebellion. There isn't a rebellion, so their sufferings can't be as terrible as you make out."

You lucky people with houses, try to work out what a monstrous piece of logic that is. An argument like that seems based on the idea that rebellion is the worst thing that can happen. Well, I can tell you—because I see it every day—that that's not true. Rebellion isn't the worst thing that can happen. True, rebellion is always a terrible thing, because those who suffer most from it are often those who were already worst off. Nevertheless, there is something worse for a nation than rebellion: it is that those who are suffering suffer so much that their sufferings are brutalising and degrading them. This brutalisation and despair, taking hold of the younger generation and of a whole people, is something much worse than rebellion.

And such is the despair and anguish of all the young people of France who, at this moment, have reached the point of founding a home. Apart from a few millionaires who can be sure of finding somewhere to live, we may say that this applies to all the young people of France, young students as much as young workers: when they come to the point when they want to start a home they have to ask themselves, in anguish, whether it is a reasonable thing to do, whether they have the right to run the risk, seeing that they do not know where they will be able to put their home and the child who may be born in it.

When the young people of a nation have got to this point, it is worse than if they rebelled.

What we need to avert rebellion is to have our young people combining with their elders to stand up and shout, peaceably but energetically: "We want houses. We want an end to the lunacy which refuses a thousand million for houses when it is well known that refusing a thousand million for houses now means agreeing to pay ten thousand million in years to come on salvaging social wrecks: ten thousand million on tuberculosis, alcoholism, lunatic asylums, prostitutes, desperate people who commit suicide, delinquent children, total down-and-outs." Every time they refuse a thousand million for housing, they are putting aside ten thousand million for criminal courts, prisons and lunatic asylums. We must understand this, and shout aloud that we've had enough of seeing things done in this absurd fashion.

POLITICAL FOLLY

Look at this, my friends. Last year, France spent a hundred and sixty-two thousand francs on trying to fight the effects of alcoholism, and, at the same time, paid out forty thousand million in subsidies for producing beetroot and other things which are no use to anyone and are being produced in too large quantity. They subsidised these useless products, which only go to produce extra alcohol, to the extent of forty thousand million francs.

Are we going to allow folly like this to go on much longer? When we came and asked for ten thousand million for emergency housing they said it was a crazy idea, that it was quite useless, that we mustn't go so fast, that in three years there would be too many houses, that we'd be seeing "to let" notices up everywhere; and they had just agreed to vote two hundred thousand million for producing alcohol and fighting alcoholism!

We must face this wretched state of affairs. Let us grasp the truth. A nation is no longer worthy of liberty, it does not deserve peace, liberty or anything else, if it is chiefly preoccupied with those who have, in general, no needs, while failing to attend to those who have so many unsatisfied needs that they are dying of them, or if it only devotes itself to them to the extent that it has something to spare after attending to the others.

THE LAW OF THE GOSPEL AND THE LAW OF ECONOMICS

If we look at it, we can see that this is an obvious matter of common sense; not only the law of the Gospel but the simplest, most elementary law of economics: any human group or community will fall a prey to suffocation and paralysis if it devotes all its productive resources to those who have no needs. And, on the contrary, it will be perpetually prosperous to the extent that it uses all the devices of government to direct production, as a matter of priority, to the service of those who lack everything. Everyone, from the bottom of the social scale to the top, finds that it pays. As soon as you get things circulating again, by creating a new market, you recreate prosperity and the nation comes alive and keeps coming alive, perpetually renewing its youth. If we are not capable of understanding this, it is because we have let ourselves get

caught and obsessed by living amongst people who have no
needs and practically never think of anyone but themselves.
If we are not capable of understanding this, it means that we
are not fit to keep our freedom. This means that, in one way
or another but all equally catastrophic, we shall be doomed to
have recourse to a brutal form of government which will seem,
in our desperate case, the only way out. And it will then be
too late for tears. We shall be driven inevitably to have recourse to tyrannous forms of government—to the worst kinds
of totalitarianism. That will be hell on earth. And we are
making straight for it if we go on in our present fashion. This
is part of the temporal as well as of the eternal law.

It is quite simple. And once you have seen it, you wonder
at how little it is realised.

PROPHECY

What we have to realise, in fact, is that the tragedy of our
world, today and in the future, consists in having lost a piece
of the machinery, so to speak, of society. The question is
whether we shall be able to act together, with the grace of
God, to re-create that piece of machinery.

What is it that our societies have lost, and for want of which
they are so fundamentally sick? What is missing from the
heart of our societies is what one might call the prophet.

The truth that I should like to make clear is that the possession of power is fated to oust the consciousness of need;
even in a man of good will, as soon as he is in power,
and however much his origins are marked by suffering and
obscurity.

Either he never leaves his original environment, so that he

has no power; he knows what the needs are, but he can do nothing about them. Or else he does attain to a certain measure of power—political, economic, financial, cultural or no matter what—and then, very soon, he is cut off from the consciousness of need.

There is a sort of curse on public office, on power. As soon as you have it, you become unconscious of real need. While he who feels the need has no power of action; at a certain level of distress he even loses the power to express himself at all.

There is no way round this, unless we can have a rebirth of something which has appeared at certain periods of history and which I will call, analogically, primitive monasticism. I mean a community of men whose vocation it is to put themselves at the heart of poverty; living in community, a community which guarantees them economic independence; living poorly, but in freedom, because of being a community, and thus able to fulfill the mission of the prophet within the city. They have the knowledge, because they are living in the same conditions as those who suffer; and they have the power of making themselves heard because they have a life in common which enables them to escape that sense of being overwhelmed which they would run the risk of bringing on themselves because of the poverty into which they are entering. They would be right in the stream of suffering without being carried away by it, and so would be able to stand up and make their voices heard.

MONASTIC REVIVAL SPLENDID BUT INCOMPLETE

We have, indeed, plenty of sanctifying communities, containing everything necessary for one's own sanctification; but

through force of circumstances these communities have got
separated from the suffering masses. There are learned men
in them. They cultivate the liturgy, and sacred art, and go in
for all sorts of scientific research; but they no longer bear
witness in the heart of the masses to the splendour of the
mysterious light of the Gospel within the human drama. The
people no longer see them living as a community before their
very eyes.

Nor do we lack plenty of militant lay people and priests,
heroic and admirable souls, who decide to plunge into the
midst of the distress of those who are suffering most; but they
are too isolated. They indeed are at the heart of distress; they
share heroically in the most horrible, the most monstrous, the
most abnormal forms of suffering which afflict the masses of
our people, but they are too much alone in it—sometimes
spiritually and almost always in their material conditions.
They are lost, carried away on the flood of distress and on the
currents of passion to which distress gives birth when it rebels.

What is lacking to our society is the presence of a *community* at the heart of the suffering masses; a presence which can
become a voice and a clamorous call to action.

Let us desire and implore God to send us plenty of volunteers, men and women, girls and boys, to dedicate themselves
to this task and this mission on a world-wide scale.

ON THE INTERNATIONAL SCALE

Moreover, our problem here is exactly the same as the
problem we find at the international level. Both in the East
and in the West we launch programmes of economic aid to
undernourished and underdeveloped populations. But this

economic aid will be no good unless the way is prepared first by people who go simply as human beings—without funds, without being labelled as officials, without careers to make for themselves—going simply out of love for men, men as men and men as the manifestation of God (ultimately one and the same love, explicit or implicit). Unless we start from the presence of such missionaries of poverty, men who come to share in the sufferings of the people, our economic programmes will do nothing (and are already doing nothing) but corrupt these backward sections of humanity, who are often very much our superiors in that they have kept the foundations of a natural morality and a natural sense of values which we have lost in the barbarism of our civilisation.

If we do not start from the presence of men coming amongst them as men to share their sufferings, all we shall be doing when we claim to raise them to a higher standard will be to reduce them to anarchy, destroying their traditional structure without being able to supply anything better to put in its place. And then, once again, the only thing for them will be to have recourse to some sort of bludgeon to deal with these anarchical passions; and we all know what tyranny leads to, no matter of what colour it may be.

I believe that these are the essential signs of the times, and that, wherever we are, each in our own town, we should be trying to act accordingly. If we succeed, there will be a tremendous upsurge of hope.

HISTORY PAST AND FUTURE

Look at history. In point of fact, whenever a civilisation has been at a crisis of mutation, faced with the necessity of assuming a new form in order to adapt itself to a totally new structure and technique, it has only succeeded in giving birth to the new civilisation which was needed by recourse to this institution of monasticism. The explanation is perfectly logical, as anyone and everyone can see. I lived for years amongst statesmen and members of Parliament, and since then I have lived in the midst of the masses; and I have seen this truth so clearly that it was simply obvious.

There are no two ways of getting political understanding. There are no two ways for a man of action, when he assumes the responsibilities of government, to arrive at understanding. There is only one. The only way of obtaining political understanding is to participate in the distress of those who are suffering most in the community which you are going to govern.

So long as you fail to understand this you will be forced to understand another truth—at our expense—which manifests itself inescapably day after day: so long as a man who is governing does not seek to acquire understanding of the problems facing him, of their relative urgency and their most needful solutions, by contact with those who are suffering, then that man may be the most intelligent and highly qualified man on earth, but we still find that he is incapable of seeing what the problems and solutions really are.

I cannot help saying this, because it is so obvious! I say it over and over again to my friends in the Government.

EUROPE

And there is, alas, a current example which is a perfect illustration of this.

Just recently Europe has been deeply divided and disturbed

by problems seriously concerning her future—problems of defence. There has been a certain amount of astonishment that things do not proceed more quickly. But how does anyone think it could be possible to accomplish, in a practical, vital sense, the profound and fundamental revolution necessary in order to create a united Europe, without the enthusiastic cooperation of the mass of workers and the mass of youth? It is perfectly obvious that it is impossible to accomplish anything of the sort unless we succeed in making the workers, and youth, enthusiastic about such a future. And, as we are all aware, with the exception of a tiny minority, the mass of workers and the mass of youth are profoundly indifferent to this immense problem. Why?

This is where we see the futility of a statesman who is not placed at the heart of those who suffer.

What is the explanation of this indifference? It is because no one has managed to give them any idea of the future except in the form of highly mysterious technical organisations, concerned with huge forces like coal and steel, in which, they are sure, it is once more a question of the interests of great financial powers and not of the real interests of the people. Again, you have presented this vast problem, this revolution of the future, in the form of military plans, making the greatest possible demands for self-denial from each individual if he is to overcome the memory of old resentments, old fears, and sufferings so recently inflicted.

What I say all the time to my friends in the Government is this: So long as you cannot point to your united Europe as, quite simply, a *building alliance,* you won't get the suffering peoples of ruined Europe—Germany, France, England, Spain, Italy, Greece, Portugal, all the nations full of homeless people —who are sceptical about your alliances, to believe enthusiastically in the future you are talking about. If you had the slightest understanding of the hearts of the people you would at least have had the elementary psychology which a primary school mistress would have had, and shown them Europe in the form of hundreds of building sites, pooling our technical resources, our labour-force, and part of our financial resources for a concerted *rebuilding* of Europe. If you had done this, then all the rest would have followed quite easily, because by building together they would have got to know and love each other in that shout of hope and joy which goes up each time a new house has been built. But it seems you couldn't realise that. And then you wonder that the people are strangers to you, you who govern them.

THE VOICE OF THOSE WHO HAVE NO VOICE

Let us try to understand these elementary things. Let us shout them at our statesmen. Let us try to tell them these simple things, because, otherwise, nothing really good will ever be done.

We have to build a world which will be a living world, not something artificial based entirely on material brute force. Of course defence forces are necessary. We have to take precautions to defend and protect what is right, but how can you expect people to want to defend their lives, their civilisation, and their society when, after a day's work, they have to crawl on all fours into a tent or go and sleep in the same room as sixteen other people?

We must begin at the beginning. But who is going to be able to say these things to the statesmen? The new monks; the men who succeed in immersing themselves in poverty without letting themselves be submerged by it, because they have the protection of their communities; men who can rise up like the prophets to hurl a challenge at the statesmen and tell them the truths which no official will ever tell them, because it isn't an official's job, nor a politician's job, nor an administrator's job. It can only be the job and the mission of a missionary of poverty, a man who is a member of a community which has decided to throw itself headlong into the heart of the problem so as to understand it, to discover some solution to it, and to put it into practice on a small scale so as to prove what can be done.

That is, basically, what the Ragpickers of Emmaus have done. A few volunteers, who came because this was what they wanted to do, became the nucleus of a swarm of desperate people. Like those who flocked to St. Benedict and St. Bernard, they provided a considerable labour-force animated by leaders whose disinterestedness was not in doubt—leaders who were able to inspire confidence in this labour force of desperate men at the heart of the greatest of the people's sufferings. They have achieved an extraordinary economic productivity, and have created whole villages, more and more of which are springing up round these communities.

By doing this, they hurled such a challenge at the people who said "It can't be done" that they turned the laws upside down, the councils of the Government upside down, the building industry upside down. They have altered the production programmes of factories; they have stimulated such bursts of generosity as in the factory which has just worked a whole day to supply us free with fifty tons of building materials. This means that eight hundred workers worked a whole day for nothing, with materials donated by the management, to supply us with fifty tons of material; twelve tons were used for building by families belonging to that factory, and thirty-eight were sent to a place near Paris for building fibro-cement huts in which we can give hundreds of families forty square yards of shelter each. We have a hundred and fifty families there already, on the grass, in tents, on a twenty-acre site which we have bought at the edge of Paris.

We have issued our challenge.

It could only have been issued by such volunteers with a following of desperate people who thus recovered hope and so, having achieved real results instead of making speeches, were in a position to open the eyes of the statesmen.

MONKS OF POVERTY, LEGIONARIES OF POVERTY

I am making this appeal to you in the name of distress throughout the whole world. I am not speaking only to you but also to all those whom you will meet tomorrow and for as long as you live. I want this appeal to go on re-echoing from you, so that we shall be given the help we need. We need to create this institute of missionaries of poverty—men who can sustain and organise a sort of legion of the desperate, a sort of Foreign Legion of volunteers who will go and join these missionaries in communities wherever demonstrations of direct action are needed to prove to the people who quibble and split hairs, by showing the movement in action, that it is not true that there is no solution.

I am counting on you, not only this evening but for the future. Help us by your prayers to obtain such vocations from God. We now consist of six hundred unfortunates, organised

by about twenty volunteers. There are plenty more who want
to come, but for that we shall need to supply sufficient organisation. Help us with your gifts. Help us, by your prayers, to
find vocations.

THE LAST JUDGMENT

I now want to say something specially to those amongst
you who are Christians, or who simply believe in something
transcending our material life. Have you seriously considered
our grave responsibilities?

Remember the Gospel. There was a day when the disciples
came and asked Our Lord concerning the Day of Judgment.
This is a serious question—the essential question. That is the
irrevocable day. How will the judgment be made which will
condemn us or save us for ever?

What does Our Lord say? What He says is extraordinary.
It is shattering. Our Lord says nothing about anything. He
says nothing about sacraments, nothing about commandments,
nothing about practices, nothing about virtues, nothing even
about prayers. He speaks only of one thing; He says: "On
that day, the Son of Man will appear in all the power of His
majesty, and He will say to some, 'I was hungry, I was cold,
I was lonely, I was homeless, and you shared what you had
with Me, you helped Me in your suffering brother. So come.'
And to others, 'You did not help Me, you did not share what
you had, so go!'"

What does it mean? What are we to make of Our Lord's
speaking of nothing but this? Does it mean that all the rest of
Our Lord's teaching is unimportant? Certainly not; His earlier
words are too clear to leave any doubt. He says, "If your eye

scandalise you, tear it out and cast it from you." Again, He
says, "Pray always," etc. Obviously all the rest is important!
But why then, when He speaks of the Judgment, the essential
summing-up, does Our Lord speak only of this one thing?

But it is perfectly clear. We must understand it. It is simply
that He wants us to understand that for Him all the other
things are only the means which He has given us to bring us
to the one thing which, for Him, counts as an end, which is
to love: to love with that true love which is, at the beginning,
a hunger and thirst for justice. This is what He wants to make
us understand—that all the other things are only *means*. And
if we have had the means but have not reached the end, then
He does not know us, for it was for that end that He gave us
the means.

A FOOLISH DEFENCE

My friends, if, on the Day of Judgment, when the Lord
says to us "Go, for you failed to share what you had with the
unfortunate," we say, in defence of ourselves, "Lord, I was a
practising Catholic, I was pious, I never missed Mass," perhaps even "I was a frequent communicant," we can be sure
of this! If we say this to the Lord to defend ourselves, when
He knows that we have not loved and have not been just,
then the wrath of the Lord will be twice as terrible. He will
say to us: "If it is true that you were a practising Catholic,
that you proclaimed yourself publicly as a friend of mine, that
you came and communicated with Me and then went out
from communicating with Me and failed to communicate to
the sufferings of your brothers—then you are twice cursed:
once because you did not help your brother, and once because,

by not doing so, you caused Me to be despised and blasphemed, by those who despised and blasphemed Me because
of you."

That is the Gospel. It is not literature or eloquence, it is
the Gospel just as it is, the Gospel raw, in the form in which
we don't want to take it, or look at it, or love it. But it is the
word of Our Lord.

Today He is silent in the tabernacle. But He has not always
been silent. Before He began to be amongst us in silence, He
spoke. Nor will He always be silent. He will speak to us again
one day, but it will not then be to teach us but to judge us.
He will not judge us by any new thing. The things which He
will say to us then will be the same things as He said to us
before, and which He wished us to be taught. It is by them
that He will judge us.

THE PUBLIC SINNERS AND THE HARLOTS WILL
GO BEFORE YOU . . .

On that Day of Judgment, the Gospel tells us, there will be
an astonishing dramatic revelation. On that day, we shall see
rising up between the Lord and ourselves more than one of
those whom we despised during our lives, more than one of
those who are now public sinners. We shall see them rising
up and saying: "Lord, there before You stands the man who
was fortunate, who went to Mass every Sunday in Your
church. . . . Oh yes," they will say, "we were the scum of
the city! Our lives were despicable and bitter and disgusting
—disgusting both to others and to ourselves. Yes, indeed, we
were wretches. But, Lord, You who know all things, You who
are just, You know that we were not always like that. There

was a time when we were boys and girls of twenty, when we had ideals and pure hearts, when we dreamt of life as something lovely; we believed in Your law, O God, we believed in our country, we believed in the people of our own time; we dared to marry and to found a home; we accepted our baby when he came—and on that day they began to throw us out of the miserable hotel room where we had taken shelter, because babies cry, and that annoys the residents. So we began to walk the streets with the baby, trying one place after another—one night with a friend, one night, now and then, in a hotel room, sometimes weeks with our parents-in-law . . . and gradually, the family began to go wrong."

The man will say: "Oh yes, Lord, I became a drunkard—a brute, perhaps, one of those child-murderers that people had to sentence from time to time." But he will go on: "Lord, what was I to do every evening, when I came back from the factory to a room full of the wife, and another family, and children everywhere? There wasn't a corner where I could sit or a chair to sit in. It got on my nerves. I got bad-tempered; I tormented my wife and thrashed the children. So it seemed better to go out. I began to go out every evening. And where could I go, three quarters of the time, except to a bar, to spend a ridiculous amount of my wages and to set about getting drunk, making myself ill, drugging myself, turning into an alcoholic, without wanting to or seeing what I was doing. What do You say I ought to have done? So I became a drunkard, an alcoholic and a madman."

And the woman will say: "I ran away in the end, because it just wasn't a life any more. A good-looking fellow came and told me a tale and I believed him and let myself be taken in. Then he deserted me. Then, so as to feed the child, whom I'd put out to a foster-mother, I began this shameful life. . . ."

"Lord," they will say, "we are guilty, indeed we are, as You know. But if, *then,* when we were twenty, when it was all just beginning, if, at that moment, there had been in our town one of these fortunate, pious people who had been willing to open his door to us; or perhaps just to risk the glossy paint of his car out of doors, and let us into his garage, so that we could put our bed and the baby's cot there . . . if there had been someone willing to do that, we should have been saved; we should have become, and remained, a fine French working-class family, with honour and joy in our lives. If we were lost, it is because there was no one willing to open his door to us, or his garage, or his loft, or his shed."

That is the truth. And that is the Gospel.

"I tell you," says Jesus, "that on the Day of Judgment the public sinners will go before you into the kingdom of heaven." On that day, if we still did not understand while there was time, the Lord will say: "My poor children, you suffered enough while you were alive. You come in first. It's your turn now. You have suffered enough. As for the others, we'll see later on, if there's still room for them." For the Lord is just, and He will render to each according to what he has done and what he has neglected to do.

WHO ARE THE BLASPHEMERS?

For it is not enough to have avoided evil; it is not enough not to have killed or stolen and so on. It is a question of what good you have done, of what you have done with the good things the Lord has entrusted to you. He did not give us wealth, education, economic position, managerial powers, or posts in trade unions or public offices so that we could minister to the desires of those who are well off; He gave us these things for the deliverance of those who are unfortunate without having deserved it. That is the function of authority, and it is upon that that God will judge us.

Sometimes we Christians mourn over the scandal of all the blasphemies that there are on earth; so many blasphemies uttered by the people, by all the peoples of the earth. . . . But so often we are hypocrites! Do you really believe that, among all these blasphemies which rise up from the earth, there are many which are real blasphemies—aimed against the true God, God as He really is, God who is Justice and Love? Do you believe that there are many people who blaspheme against God as the God of Justice and the God of Love? You know very well they don't. Of course, amongst the workers as elsewhere, there are people who utter real blasphemies, but it isn't as many as one in ten. There are fewer real blasphemies amongst the people than amongst the intellectuals. There are very few real blasphemies. The vast majority of these curses are false blasphemies—blasphemies hurled against God, not as He is, but as we have caricatured Him, as our way of living shows Him.

But if, in our way of living, we are able to live at last as real Christians; if we are able, in our life as Christians and as communicants, to communicate in the suffering of others, to share with our brothers; if we are able to imitate Our Lord, whose face is the face of love hungering and thirsting for justice—then, we may be sure, it is not blasphemies which will be uttered by the workers, from amongst whom Our Lord chose the best of His apostles.

For it was from amongst the little people that Our Lord chose to take His first apostles. Out of all the twelve, there was one office worker, St. Matthew, and all the others were labourers, and very poor labourers at that. And all down the centuries, Our Lord has indeed found His priests in all walks of life, but He has never ceased to find hosts of them amongst the humblest of the workers.

Those who suffer will blaspheme no longer once we succeed, by our way of living, in showing them our true face as children of God, the true face of the Lord. On that day there will arise, instead of blasphemies, songs of peace and of joy, of love and of justice.

PAX!

You see, we all want peace. But if we are to have peace, we must first do battle in ourselves for justice. It is only when we do justice that God will give peace by granting understanding to our governments.

TO THE JUNIOR SEMINARY
AT ROUEN*

THE "BATTLE OF THE SEMINARY"

There are so many things to say to you, my friends! I do
not know which to choose, with so little time in which to
speak to you this morning.

Whenever I am asked if I can come to a seminary, whether
a major seminary or junior seminary, I always say yes, because
I remember my own years at college, and afterwards in the
Capuchin novitiate and scholasticate. I know how hard and
difficult a time it is, and how, if you are to hold on and be
strong, you need to have your heart and mind constantly
filled with everything which relates to God—anything by
which we can know God in this world.

Later on, when it is your turn, never forget that it is your
duty to help those who have taken your places in the impatient world of the seminary.

"IF GOD DOES EXIST, IT'S THE SORT OF THING
YOU'RE DOING"

Today, I only want to tell you one thing. You will be able
to reflect more deeply on it as you advance in your vocation.

* 15th of October, 1954.

110

Amongst the means which there are of knowing God in this world, and so of making Him known, the most infallible and powerful is to love all unfortunate people in a genuine, practical, active way.

One Saturday evening four years ago someone brought me a small hut which had been dismantled and which was being presented to me as a shelter for a family. It was very late. We needed some cement blocks to put under the floor of this hut so that it wouldn't rot. As it was Saturday, the builders were all closed, and we hadn't enough blocks. It looked as if we might be going to lose a lot of time, because Sunday was the only day when there were enough of us free to build this house quickly. While I was worrying over this, one of my friends said, "You know, there's an old navvy down the road who makes cement blocks at home in wooden frames so as to earn a bit of cash. You'd better go and see; I'm sure he'll let you have some." I went straight off in the car, with a trailer for the stuff we wanted. I knocked at his door; a little boy answered it. This little boy shouted, "Daddy, it's Abbé Pierre," and the man of the house appeared. He was getting on in years, but a great, strapping fellow for all that. He came with grave solemnity, as is always the way in a working-class family on any serious occasion, and said, "Come in, monsieur l'Abbé." He gave me a chair, and a drink, and then said: "Monsieur l'Abbé, you are the first priest I have let into my house." I said to myself, "This is a good beginning; I seem to have got the wave-length. What happens now?" So then this good soul started pouring his whole heart out in a long monologue. He said, "Things can't really be the way *they* do them." He didn't say, "the way they *say*"—meaning religious people. Then he came out with all the criticisms, which we have to admit, in honesty, are well deserved—the things which scandalise all poor and unfortunate folk. Amongst others, he talked about that notorious business which, I am glad to say, has changed a lot and changes more all the time: how scandalous he thought it when some man dies, and they organise a great deal of fuss, with plenty of solemnity, even if everyone knows that he was a thorough rogue—that he was dishonest in business, that he led his family a miserable life, that he was unfaithful to his wife, that he was a bad man all round—just so long as he's a rich man; if so, the Church will give him plenty of solemn ceremony. Then he went on: "And if, the same day, there's some poor mother, some poor old woman whom everyone admires, who's been a perfect model all her life, then they're in a great hurry, they've no time for her, they do it all in five minutes, just because she hasn't a penny." In short, he gave me the works, just like that—everything he had in mind. And at one point he banged on the table and said, "And all the same, I'd like to be able to get to know God," rather as if he meant: "I'd like to have a discussion with someone who'd be serious about it, who'd understand what I have in my heart, what it is I mean, what ideals of goodness and justice I have in my heart."

So he went on talking. And when he'd finished, I started. I answered as well as I could. And then I explained that I'd come for some concrete blocks. We talked about it all. He said that what I was doing was a good thing; housing people who haven't any houses, who haven't any money; that, he said, was why he let me in—but he wouldn't ever let one of those "priests" in. In the end, he gave me the blocks. It was ten o'clock by then. I went off in the night, and—now, listen: I have told this story in lots of seminaries, and before cardinals, and before the Nuncio, and before bishops, and in many different countries—that old workman, that good old soul, who'd spent three quarters of an hour blaspheming and talking irreligion and everything you can think of, when we were saying good-bye in the street, beside the car, he put his hands on my shoulders and said a terrific thing: "Well, look, after all, Abbé, maybe if God does exist, it's this sort of thing that you're doing."

Do you see the meaning of those clumsy, tremendous words?

"If God does exist, it's the sort of thing you're doing" means that He is the power by which you give a roof to the suffering and bread to the hungry, by which you befriend the unfortunate and share the suffering of others; the source of all love.

That man wasn't a theologian or a philosopher, but he said something of the utmost profundity. God is not a theory or a system. Either God does not exist, or else He is Love: eternal, living Love, manifesting itself throughout creation, throughout all of us, so as to make the world into a communion, a communion of men with each other, as an image of Himself; as one of the ways He has of expressing what He is in the eternal Trinity of Persons: the Love which is interior to God, the love of the Father, the Son and the Spirit; that Love which overflows in creation, which overflows in Redemption, which brings Him to make Himself man, to become a little baby crying in the straw, and then to spend His whole life in poverty and labour and at last to die between *hardened criminals.* . . .

That was our Lord's life. And it was love which led to all that, for the ransoming of sins, which are failures in love.

For all sins are failures in love. They are the refusal to love, the refusal to be united with those who are around us. Sin always means taking ourselves, our own ego, as the centre of everything. *I* am the only one who counts. But the moment there is love and a real self-giving, that is really the end of sin and reparation for sin. This going out of oneself, this self-giving to others, is really the foundation of everything.

The first condition for understanding anything of God, for knowing Him and showing Him to others, is to look at all the suffering there is in the world, beginning with your "neighbour."

OUR NEIGHBOUR

At this point, I should like to consider another idea with you.

In the Gospel, God does not speak to us of "others." He speaks of our "neighbour." You people who know Latin must be aware of the difference between *alter* and *proximus*. *Alter* is just the second in line, the one who comes next, and that's that. There's the first and the second, the one who happens to be just there. But God does not speak in this way. When He wishes to speak of whom we are to love, He says we are to love our neighbour. What does it mean?

"Neighbour" means a relationship, and there's no end to it. "Others" is limited. "Neighbour" is infinite. In a hierarchical arrangement, your neighbour is the nearest. But there is no limit to the "nearest." It reaches from "nearest" to "nearest," to the ends of the earth. The nearest to *you*, for a start, are your father and mother, your brother, your friend, your teacher, the people in your town, in your own country, and the neighbouring countries. But, going from one "nearest" to another, it reaches to the ends of the earth.

The love of God, which He came to bring us, which He wishes us to have in our hearts, ought to embrace the whole world; and at the same time, we ought to start fulfilling it, without any romanticising, in whatever is nearest, whatever we can do most immediately and most quickly.

The best and first way for us to know God is to listen to that voice within us, which we know is the best of all voices, which is His own voice, and which says: "Forget yourself. Forget your own pleasure and your egotism, and accept whatever sacrifice is necessary in order to go and love your neighbour entirely, starting from whoever is nearest, and especially those who have the most need, being the most unhappy. Look at Jesus. He loved, first of all, those who were most unhappy."

PAUPERES EVANGELIZANTUR

You know the story in the Gospel of how the disciples of the prophet John the Baptist came to question Jesus. "Tell us who you are. Are you the one we are waiting for? Are you the Messiah, the centre of world history, the one who has been foretold down the centuries? Or are you simply one link in the great chain leading up to the Messiah? Or are you yourself the Messiah?" What is Our Lord's wonderful answer? He says simply: "Go and tell your master—and by this sign he will know; he will recognise Me and know that I really am the Messiah—go and tell him that all those who are afflicted are being succoured and loved; go and tell him that *pauperes evangelizantur,* that the poor are receiving joy, the good news, the proclamation of the good news. Till now, philosophers and wise men have concerned themselves with those who could study, with people who were very intelligent and very rich, so that they were capable of studying. But I am he who proclaims the good news to the poor, to the little people, to

man for his own sake, without minding whether he is rich, or
has a degree, or the right clothes, but just man, in all his
poverty and littleness."

LOVE DESIRES LIKENESS

The knowledge we must have of God is not a knowledge of
ideas, an intellectual knowledge, but the knowledge you have
of a friend, your own friend, your best friend. You only know
him if you live as he does, act as he does, try to love as he
does. If you want to know Jesus, and know God through Him,
you must look at what He was like, model your heart on His
and apply yourself to loving as He loved, to knowing those
who suffer so as to love them as He loved them.

The more you prepare yourselves for this, think about it,
reflect on it, and try, in your studies and reading, to learn to
understand suffering and poverty and how to act to relieve it,
the more you will be able to know God intimately, not only
as an idea but in His very Being; you will begin to become
His friend, to grow like Him and to be united with Him. This
really is the primary way of knowing God.

Do you know this? At this moment in the world, as we
learn from the latest official statistics produced by the United
Nations special commissions, nearly half the human beings
living on this globe are without homes. By a home we mean a
place where a family can be on its own, and not live like
animals in a stable. If we take account of China, Africa,
India, South America, and the working-class population of all
our great industrial cities, where two, three or even four
families are piled one on top of each other in one apartment,
half the human beings in the world have no roof of their own

The Emergency Village at Noisy, in its first days. Today it shelters 250 families (with 1,000 children), as they wait for permanent homes.

Abbé Pierre with the children of the homeless.

over their heads. And this is an age when we have all the technical means to work miracles, if we wanted to! But men are such fools that they never think of making this their starting-point.

Do you know that three-quarters of the people in the world today do not have the minimum food to eat on which you can grow to be a fully adult human being? Three-quarters of the inhabitants of the world are undernourished, simply haven't enough—while we constantly waste food. Do you know this— I heard it at a congress in Germany: a Japanese expert was giving us an enormous amount of information about many countries, and he told us that there are certain areas of Asia where laws or administrative decisions have been made forbidding the vaccination of babies, because it is less agonising to see children dying of disease than of hunger! That is happening in the world today.

We have to know these things; otherwise we are not Christians, we are only thinking of ourselves and our own little affairs, even if we rise to thinking about our country and our country's affairs. There is something badly wrong with the world, for these things are abominable. We have to live with this realisation, if we want to be truly Christian.

There is something I dream of seeing in every house, rich or poor, especially in schools and most of all in seminaries, in the place of honour, the most important place in the house, the place where the household gathers together. It can take an artistic form in a luxurious room, or simply be a sheet of paper in a humbler house: a map of the world. I dream of seeing Christian households, which say their prayers, having this map as the place where they put their statue of Our Lady and the Child Jesus, and the crucifix. I dream of seeing the fathers and mothers in these Christian households, when they

have evening prayers and bring their children to pray in front
of Our Lord and Our Lady, have them say their prayers in
front of this map of the world. And, according to the age of
the children, and basing themselves on the day's news, they
will say: "Look at this place, Calcutta. Every day they have
carts which go along the streets in the morning to pick up
those who haven't got onto their feet, who have died of hunger
in the night. . . . In other parts of the world, there are boys
of your age, twelve or fourteen years old, who work for ten
or twelve hours a day just to have something—barely that—
to wear and to eat; and they work in these conditions so that
we can have iron and tin cheap, and so have the possibility of
a pleasanter way of life. There are places where people work
in frightful conditions at extracting rubber so that *we* shall
have enough rubber to go gadding about in cars and have
trucks for our work. But *they* don't get enough by it to live in
a way fit for men." And so on, with other problems all over
the world.

We need to live thus haunted by the worst misfortunes that
there are in the world. It is to these sufferers that you should
go first with your witness to the Gospel, if you want to be
heard by all, both poor and rich. This does not mean that
Jesus only came to save the poor. He came to save both rich
and poor. He came to save everyone. But God knows what
He is about! He does not need instructions about the best way
of doing things. He knows what He has to do! And He, who
came to save everyone, rich and poor alike, He, the Son of
King David, who could have been born in some other period
when he would have been rich and powerful, He who, with
all His human and divine intelligence, could have put Himself in a position which would have been *both* holy *and* important and dazzling—what did He choose? To save both

rich and poor, He chose to be poor, even to be the poorest of the poor. If He chose it, He knew what He was doing. He wished to be poor because He knows that, if the poor are to believe you, you must be like them, you must share their sufferings; whereas for the rich to take you seriously, you don't have to be like them!

I have often said this before. When I found that mother living in a tent who had lost two of her three children, it was the most terrible day of my life as a priest. I realised that if I were going to preach, and talk about morality to that mother, and didn't give up my place in my house to her, I was nothing but a humbug; I wouldn't be able to talk to her about God any more.

I realised that if I wanted to stir up rich people about it, fortunate people, people who were in a position to give her a room and save the baby she was expecting, there was only one way to do it. The only way was to give an example; to take those people and say, "Go and sleep in my bed," and to take their place myself. And then to go next day to the rich, fortunate people, not to lecture them but to say, "This is what happened."

It was not possible to leave that mother there with the baby that was going to be born. As long as it was just one poor woman, everyone shut their eyes to it, no one paid any attention. But because I, a priest, did this scandalous thing to bring shame on those who had the means, things began to happen.

The explanation of what happened last winter—the sort of storm which shook everybody, rich and poor alike—is that people acted in this way. They didn't preach or produce fine phrases; they did what they could, trying to live the Gospel as Our Lord would have done. And it shook the world, because to convert the poor you must be like them. And to convert the rich you must be unlike them. That is what Our Lord knew. And that is what He did, not because He didn't want to save the rich, but in order to save them.

When you have a rich, well-fed priest—what I am going to say now is terrible, but it is true—you can be sure that there are whole pages of the Gospel which he will never preach, because he can't. There are things in the Gospel which, if he says them as they are, will make everyone smile and say: "Quite so. That's a sermon, of purely literary value; but we know very well how he lives, he never denies himself anything. So he can tell us as much as he likes that that's the Gospel. . . ."

A priest *must* love poverty, because it is only then that people will believe him when he says that he loves God; for God is Love, and Love consists in sharing with those who suffer. You cannot pretend that you are loving when you share the condition of those who have a superabundance of everything and are not struggling to serve those who suffer; that is being, not a lover, but an accomplice. Love means sharing with those who suffer.

That was the first thing I wanted to say to you.

The second thing is that you must be patient.

I know of the hours when patience is needed. There are times, during the years when you are preparing to be a priest, when it seems as though it were going on for ever, as though you were never going to be done with wearing out your pants sitting at desks. You want to be doing something! You want to start straight away! You are impatient to be at your vocation, whatever it is. There are times when you are completely fed up!

Believe me. I am speaking from experience. In this improbable life that I've been living the past fifteen years, a crazy life, in which—as I realise more every day—you have every chance of getting completely played out—if I have more or less stuck it out, if I'm not finished, when I have scarcely any time or strength for reading, with life as full and exhausting as it is, and so many bewildering affairs sending me here, there and everywhere—if I've managed to hold out and can go on, it is because during all my years in the Order I had so much time for prayer. Between singing the Office in choir and having one hour of prayer at night and one hour in the evening, we had a total of almost seven hours of prayer, day and night, for eight years. And all the rest of the time we were meditating, and living in poverty. We prayed more than we studied, for conditions were not very favourable for first-class studying. True, I suffered from this then, and I think things could have been better managed.

But I have understood since that we did not lack the most essential thing, the most important: those hours of prayer, when you suffer, and you think about God, you reflect on God and think over what you have read in the Gospel and learnt in your studies. During that time of prayer and patience something gets graven very deeply into us.

Now, living with my ragpickers, we have a slogan which they know well, because I am always repeating it; for they too have their sorrows and sufferings—there are six hundred and fifty of us now, living in common round Paris—they have their hours of despair. There is a plank in my office—there being more planks than fine furniture where I live—on which hangs a great array of knives. One of them is bloodstained. I drew it out of the breast of one of my friends who tried to kill himself one night in a moment of despair. The others are knives which some of the lads pulled on each othei in quarrels. There's one which one of them tried to use on me. Next day he wept and begged for forgiveness. In the midst of their suffering and despair there is this slogan which they know well: they often hear me say it: "You know, old man, you don't make the corn grow faster by pulling on the blade." It needs time. It needs rain. It needs sun. It needs cold. It needs snow. It needs warmth. Then, when the time is ripe, there is corn; and after that, bread. It needs time. And so it is with salvation, and with one's vocation.

So, have trust in God.

When you are at the end of your tether, go to your spiritual director. Storm at him, if it does you any good: "I've had enough," etc., etc.—tell him what's on your mind. And when you've got it off your chest, take heart and say to yourself, "It'll be over sometime." The time for external action will come. And it is now, while you dig the foundations of your interior life, that you are preparing for it.

Today, when I am applauded on all sides, with everyone saying, "The Abbé Pierre is wonderful, he's terrific, he's a real priest, he's a real Christian, if only everyone were like him. . . ." I firmly believe that it is not I who have merited all these things. It is like the candles on the altar. If the sacristan has lit one of them, and it catches everyone's eye because it has been lit, that doesn't mean that it is better than the others, which haven't been lit. Next day perhaps a different one will be lit (indeed, it will be, so as to keep them all about the same length!). God acts in the same way.

If there is good being done today; if there are people who had rebelled and blasphemed against God in their despair, and who have found God again because of things that my companions and I are doing, I have few illusions about the foundations of it. I am sure that it is due, not to us—for it is much more a question of "what happens to us" than of "what we do"; it is not we who have chosen, but events which have made things happen—but it is due to a multitude of unknown souls who attract no attention at all, but who pray and offer themselves in sacrifice. There are all the nuns in their convents, unknown to anyone; there are mothers in their kitchens, in wretched houses, darning socks for their sons and husbands —which is no joke—who never go to the films, who have no money to spend on entertainment, and who do their duty and pray to God. There are your mothers. And there are all of you, in your Junior Seminary. There are boys and girls in schools and everywhere else, praying and offering and making sacrifices.

That is what makes it possible for those who are in the thick of the fight to have the grace of God and to do a little good. And that is what will give you the courage to prepare yourselves for tomorrow.

Those were the two chief things which I wanted to say to you today.

First: Love those who are the least, and the poorest, and the most unhappy. There you can be sure of making no mistake. However much you are sinners, however hopeless characters you may be, it is impossible that God will not be with you. If you are always amongst those who love the poor, who live with the poor, who are in communion with those who suffer most, it is not possible that you will not be in communion with God. He said it a hundred times, in different ways, in the Gospel. The best way of knowing if we are in communion with God is to see whether we are in communion with the sufferings of men.

Second: Remember the necessity for patience, patience in prayer, in work, in sacrifice.

If you do that, I do not know what you will be; I do not know whether you will be the lighted candle or the candle dumped in a corner, whether you will be on the high altar or on a side altar; it simply does not matter. What is certain is that tomorrow you will be truly the hands of God penetrating this unhappy world. You will be the face of God. And you will make God loved. And you will give men hope. And you will save all those people who are, after all, just as good as we, but who simply have not had what we have had.

It is like the story of the talents. We do not have them for ourselves. We have them to make them fruitful for the profit of others.

So, since we have been given all this, let us go to work. Let us work with Our Lord. Remember that He is with you, in the measure in which you love each other and prepare yourselves to understand and study the suffering of the whole world. Don't only study the geography of wealth and glory and power; study human geography—the real totality of human geography. Get your teachers to tell you about the kinds of poverty characteristic of each part of the world—of each part of the world and of each part of our towns and parishes. Let it open your hearts to a truly catholic, universal view of this world, the *whole* of which Jesus desired to save.

There.

I beg you to pray for us often, my companions and me; it is gruelling work, and no fun at all. Think of us sometimes. And pray.

Let us pray for all those men of good will who might perhaps have been real apostles, with the great souls that they have, if the Christians had been more Christian, and had managed to show them, by their example, what a marvellous thing it would be for them to follow Our Lord.

And now, please, let us say one "Hail Mary" to Our Lady to put it all into her hands: your vocations, and all the work of Jesus through the hands of His Church.

AT THE "MAISON DU LOGEMENT" 32, RUE DES BOURDONNAIS,*

We wanted to meet today, my friends, to commemorate that extraordinary 1st of February that we had last year.

There is one small point about it which I want to consider with you; it may seem a detail to some, but not to me; and probably it will be the same for many of you, indeed all of you, when you have thought about it.

This morning we met together in prayer. And we found that the passages we had to read at Mass were wonderfully applicable to our own lives, having been chosen for their application to the life of John Bosco, a recent, modern saint, not from some remote period, but quite close to us in many ways; a man who devoted his life to work very like that which we are trying to do.

Yet, when we met this morning we were, really, anticipating.

What exactly was the time of the outbreak now known as "the rising of the 1st of February"? You will see, if you examine it, that it was launched on the Radio at one o'clock in the afternoon. One-thirty to two o'clock was the time taken by that record-breaking explosion—the shock which did not

---

* 1st of February, 1955.

merely bring about some astonishing material results but which penetrated deeply into the souls of no one knows how many people. It echoed through the world, and stirred something—more here, less there—and revived something fresher, younger, newer, purer, nearer to what God meant when He created the world, in the hearts of millions of people, if only for a moment.

So the whole explosion really took place, if we look at the Church's liturgy, at the time of the first vespers—the beginning of any important feast, which starts on the afternoon of the previous day—the first vespers of *Our Lady's Feast on the 2nd of February, the Feast of her Purification and of the Presentation of the Child Jesus in the Temple.*

It happened on the Feast of the 2nd of February, Candlemas, the feast of innocence and humility, the feast of Sacredness at its most sacred. On this day Our Lord, the infinite, wholly sacred Word of the eternal God, God Himself, came, because He wanted to become one of us, came in His humanity to be presented by the hands of His mother in a public, external gesture of oblation; to be presented in the Temple by the hands of the Virgin Mary to the Lord, His Father, in the first public act of consecration of His holy humanity for the redemption of all of us, the mass of sinful humanity.

And while it is thus the feast of Our Lord's humility, it is also the feast of Our Lady's humility. For the religious ceremony of the purification of a mother after childbirth, as prescribed by the old law of Israel, was a religious rite which was an act of penance, expiation and reparation for any guilt or sin which might be in her.

And here we have the holy and immaculate Virgin, sinless and faultless in all her life, choosing to be like others when she was so far above others, and to do as everyone else did. More-

over, she wished to perform this act as one of the least among
the people; for, as you know, at this ceremony of Purification
and Presentation, a victim had to be offered at the Temple to
have its throat cut in sacrifice. And because she was poor, Our
Lady came bringing a pair of turtle-doves—pigeons. This was
the offering of the poor, of those who simply could not bring
anything better. So the Blessed Virgin came, she who was of
royal race and the Mother of God, like any ordinary mother,
and a very poor mother at that.

When I think of this offering at the Temple at Jerusalem,
I often go on to think of a point in the Gospel which suddenly struck me one day not so long ago. It happened to be
this particular passage of the Gospel at Mass that morning; it
was in the chapel at Neuilly-Plaisance, and suddenly this detail struck me. It was the day when Our Lord was driving
the money-changers from the Temple. He was carried away
by real anger. There is nothing symbolic about this anger. The
Gospel says that He picked up some cords for a whip, and
used them. Those were not blows from symbolical cords. It
was real. It happened like that. And then, the Gospel tells us
—and this is beautiful—"The money of the changers he
poured out, and the tables he overthrew." Think of that sight!
All thrown on the ground and rolling all over the place. It
wasn't paper, it was gold coins! It must have rolled everywhere! And there was plenty of it. It was an enormous trade,
a sort of banking business there in the entrance to the Temple.
He turned it all upside down. Imagine what a scene it must
have been afterwards, with everyone trying to recover his
own. . . . And what fun for any scavenging ragpickers who
happened to be there. Then, the Gospel says, "When he had
made, as it were, a scourge of little cords, he drove them all
out of the temple, the sheep also and the oxen." This was a

huge trade. It was run by great cattle-merchants, sellers of prize beasts, who did their trade there by providing offerings for the people who came, day after day, from far off, from the ends of Israel, sometimes in rich caravans, to buy these animals for sacrifice. The Temple trade in Jerusalem was something vast! And now comes the delightful touch: after showing His anger in this violent way, by force and brutality —for it is brutal to drive animals with blows of a whip and to overturn people's tables—the Gospel says: "And to them that sold doves he said: Take these things hence."

For the smaller people who were there too, the poorer, lesser folk, there was no anger. He is here, and He is not going to let them do what is not fitting, but He does not scold them. There is no more anger. These are little people. He tells them to go, and He educates and instructs them by explaining, "Do not make the house of prayer into a den of thieves." But there is no more violence.

So every time I think of those turtle-doves, I remember all this.

We must understand what Our Lady wanted to do. She wanted to make her offering in the midst of everyone, and at the level of the least of the people; and, with herself, to put Jesus Himself at that lowest level for all of us.

Here you have the delicacy of a totally Christian soul, loving and desiring to love. So long as we put it in its true light, it can never be possible to say too much about how vast and extraordinary, when you think about it, is the part played by Our Lady in our lives as men. In all the rough harshness of human existence, Our Lady's presence amongst us is something immeasurable and extraordinary. She is someone just like us, who lived just as we do, in the midst of the apostles —who were not, be it noted, milk-and-water choir boys, but argued amongst themselves, with quarrels between St. Peter and St. Paul, and so on. After all, they were people with tempers, and they were a cross to one another. And Our Lady lived in the midst of them all. Amongst them, she was light at its most human; God shining through amidst human beings; God present through her gentleness and goodness. . . .

What the Blessed Virgin must have suffered is something tremendous.

She saw these men whom Our Lord had gathered together, whom He had made subject to Himself, and who, by His grace, had come near to Him. They were sailors; they didn't turn into saints the day they joined Our Lord. We need only look at what happened at the moment of crisis; they all, without exception, left Him. So they weren't saints—in the sense of being impeccable, I mean. They *were* saints, and they became great saints, through the energy and courage with which they fought all their lives, constantly renewing their efforts to be like Our Lord, and finally giving up life itself. But it wasn't sanctity made in advance, prefabricated, without having to be fought for! And we can imagine Our Lady, with her sensitivity, in the midst of these rough people. It certainly cannot always have been very enjoyable; she must have had many tears to shed, and many quarrels and ruptures to put right, with many occasions for scolding, reproving and correcting, as a mother does—as I often say—encouraging, not discouraging, but reproving and correcting all the same.

And consider this: at the moment when they all ran away, when they were scattered, it is possible—we don't know for certain, but it is very probable—that there was a moment when they all completely lost their faith; when they were shattered by seeing that Our Lord had been crucified, that He had not been able to use His tremendous powers, that He had

not worked a miracle to deliver Himself, but had let Himself
be executed like a brigand. In their bewilderment, it is very
likely that, at one time or another, they all reached the point
of not knowing what to think. There was probably a day—
the Saturday between the death of Our Lord and His resurrection—when the whole faith of the Church, faith in Jesus
the incarnate Son of God, had no existence except in the heart
of the Virgin Mary. It is probable that during that Saturday,
during those hours of general bewilderment until they gathered round her again at the cenacle, it was in her alone, in her
heart alone, that the whole faith of the new-born Church on
earth subsisted.

So, in all our difficulties, in all our struggles and our times
of weariness, let us look at Our Lady and say: We are no
more than we are, and that isn't much; we are like children,
but you know us as a mother knows her children. What a
mother looks for is not whether her child has done much or
little of what he ought not to have done, but whether he
wants to be a good child or not. If he does, his mother doesn't
worry; but neither has she any illusions. When a child comes
and says, "Mummy, I've been naughty, I won't be again,"
she knows very well that he'll be doing something similar
tomorrow, that he will go on for years like that, and that he
will be hurting her all her life. But because she sees that he
wants to be good she keeps on trusting, and the more difficulties and troubles she has with him the more she loves him.

So we will be like that with Our Lady. We will trust her
with everything, and what does everything mean? It means
the task which has been thrust upon us. As with the apostles,
it was not really we who chose it. The apostles were not looking for Our Lord. It was He who passed by, and said to each
of them, in one way or another, "Come. Will you come?"

And so He gathered them together, one after the other. But these men, good fellows though they were, were also sinners like anyone else, and they weren't expecting anything of this sort.

Exactly like ourselves, on the eve of the 1st of February.

Most of us could not have foreseen, the day before or an hour before, that we were going to find ourselves launched on this mad course that was to eat up our days and nights and set its mark on our whole lives to the very day of our death and the last breath we draw; for there are things of such a nature that they set a mark upon us which nothing can efface.

It is not possible that the things we have lived through should be as though they had never existed. We may fall into sin again, do stupid things, be hopeless people, or any thing you like; but something has left its mark on us which can never cease to exist.

It is so with all our comrades in the communities. How often I have seen it and said it! Even when—and it happens everywhere, in our communities as everywhere else—some of them go back to doing stupid things, to gravely sinful things— I know of examples of this, over the years—there is never a case of a person who doesn't sooner or later give some sign, in some act, which shows that something remains to him of his life in the community. He is not the same as he was before. He may still be, or become, a wretched, miserable sort of person. But there is something in him which cannot be effaced. He has been bathed in a life which is not, indeed, perfect, but of which the principles are perfect.

It isn't that we are better than other people, but that the foundations on which we try, in our poor way, to organise our life—our life in community, our life in the city, our life in all its forms—are foundations of absolute truth, because they are the practical application of that commandment which is the law of life and death for every society and every soul: Love.

And "love" translated into practice means this: to put first whoever is suffering most, to make those who are suffering our first care and our first preoccupation in every possible way. Until we have understood that, the formula about "loving your neighbour as yourself" is simply a joke. Either loving your neighbour as yourself means nothing at all, or else it means that I must attend to anyone who is less fortunate than I, and that I must attend first and primarily to him. The least happy person is the person to attend to first—this is what it is to love him as oneself—so that he too can come to have his own vocation and his own particular way of life—that full human development which is what I want for myself. It won't come in the same way for everyone; for each, it will correspond to what he himself is.

And this is the foundation of our whole life: to serve, and to serve first those who are suffering most.

And so, even though we are feeble creatures no better than others and perhaps less good, because we have freely chosen to give our lives this basic direction we have been able to do fine and good things; not because we are better, but because our foundations are solid and true, so that *they are* better. We may be miserable people, but if we adopt this as our rule of life, and constantly try to come back to it as our rule of life, we shall do amazing things.

There is a staggering sentence in the Gospel. Our Lord says to His disciples, "You have seen great things, but if you live according to this law you shall do even greater things than I have done Myself!" Our Lord said that to His disciples. "You shall do greater things than I have done." And it is true, because what we shall have then will be the fullness of Our Lord acting as one with the whole human community living in communion with Him. Such is the power of the whole Christ, the whole humanity of the Son of God, complete— Christ who is both the head and the body; then, in the fullness of His stature and His power, the whole Christ will be able to fulfill even greater tasks, acting throughout the world and all down the centuries.

This is our task.

Let us ask Our Lady to take us just as we are, to take us by the hand and scold and correct us, not to throw us into despair, but to encourage us when we need it. Let us ask her, in the worst of all weariness which is weariness of oneself, in those moments when we are sad because we see that we do not do what we wish to do, when we want to be impeccable and find that we are still poor sinners—for the greatest of all discouragements is to recognise that we are not what we would wish to be—let us ask her to prevent us from being discouraged, and to give us—understanding, for understanding is a virtue! And in a mission and a task like ours, the two principal virtues are courage and understanding. Courage even when things are hard. And understanding to see what needs to be done. Courage always has value in itself, but God grant that we may apply it to the full to whatever is most effectively urgent at any particular moment. Let us ask for this. Let us ask Our Lady for it. She will have been a good housewife; she must have had a practical mind. She knew how to manage what had to be done. Let us ask her to help us in this, and not to allow us to get discouraged. May she make us see the smallest tasks that need to be done here, at once, at our

very feet; and at the same time the huge dimensions of the
task that needs to be done throughout the world.

May Our Lord help us both to be practical in small, daily
things—making a good job of typing a letter, or sorting our
rubbish bins, or whatever we have to do here and now—and,
at the same time, to say to ourselves constantly: there is a tremendous task to be done throughout the whole world, and in
that we have to be one little spark amongst others, so that
other people can catch fire from our spark.

Through Our Lord, it is possible.

When we look at it. . . . There was a time not long ago
when there was nothing. There was a time when there were
two of us . . . a time when there were four or five of us.
How many are we today? I don't know the total. There are
certainly more than eight hundred people in the communities.
With the committees and everything else, how many militants
must there be, in towns which we don't even know? And how
many people have been aroused by our example, and are
working today? And how much is done through the review?
The propaganda experts tell me (and they say that no adver-
tiser has ever achieved so much) that it is possible to estimate
that, taking into account the press, radio, motion pictures,
television, and everything else, about half the human race has
received some sort of impact from us! A thousand million
human beings, from one end of the world to the other! Copies
of the review have gone off by aeroplane to the North Pole,
and stayed there. There are people who have seen them, and
read them, and come back. We have had letters from New
Zealand. About a fortnight ago, at Laghet, at the little shrine
of Our Lady where I was resting, I received a money order

for thirty thousand francs via the governor of the territory of
the Upper Volta. A football team in Wagadugu had had a
game and sent me the gate money. This in itself is something
memorable. In an age when colonies and colonial powers are
at daggers drawn all over the world, when there is no agree-
ment or understanding, with one side refusing to give enough
responsibility and the other side demanding more and more,
when, in short, there is a mass of highly complicated problems, it is staggering that a little thing like this should be able
to flower. These Africans—and God knows what poverty and
need they are in—sending something to help us to do what
we are doing here: it's miraculous! And things like that are
coming in from all over the world.

So we must understand the scope of our responsibilities.
And we must have confidence, with Our Lady's help.

NOTRE-DAME DE LAGHET*

DISILLUSIONMENT

During these days, my brethren, we are beginning the season of Lent; the time during which we should be preparing ourselves for that mighty event upon which we may say that the whole of human history turns—the whole history of the universe and of man: the Resurrection, the Resurrection of Our Lord and, through Him and in Him, the resurrection of man—the defeat of nothingness, the defeat of death, the victory of life, forever.

Like all our life on earth, and like each of the divisions of the liturgical year, this time is really a time of waiting, of preparation and of hope.

And it needs, too, to be a time of disillusionment; a time when we go out from our illusions to encounter reality, and to encounter life. It is a time which should prepare us for something to happen in us similar to what happened to those few men who had been Our Lord's fervent disciples, and who had seen the horrible tragedy of Maundy Thursday night and of Good Friday.

They had seen their Lord arrested, mocked, tortured, executed. They had seen Him—Him, whose power and splendour

---

* February 1955.

137

and authority they had seen manifested during His three years
of public life and fame—perishing, a helpless victim, torn and
bleeding. They had seen Him let Himself be put to death
between hardened criminals.

THE DISCIPLES AT EMMAUS

Think of their utter bewilderment.

You know this story in the Gospel—at once so staggering
and so full of poetry. It was the Sunday after the Passion,
and on one of the roads in the outskirts of Jerusalem two men
were walking along. They were running away. They were
scared of everything. They said to themselves that all those
who were known to have been near to Our Lord were doubt-
less going to be persecuted by the authorities and the police.
They had only one idea in their heads: to get away.

A week before, these men had experienced all the extraordinary enthusiasm of Palm Sunday. They had witnessed the
acclamation by the people of *their* Lord—the man whose companions they had been for months and perhaps for years—in a
sort of equivalent of a triumphal procession down the
Champs-Elysées. And then, with brutal suddenness, came the
collapse of all their hopes.

Can you think of any greater and more perfect hopes than
theirs had been? They lived under a foreign occupation. This
was going to be liberation. He had such moral power, such
power over the crowds, such authority in every sense—and,
seeing that He was of the family of David, it was obvious that
He was the leader and king who had been foretold—both that
He would be able to bring them liberation and—since He was
so holy that no one had ever known anyone so holy, and

reasonable, and sane, and wise—that He would set up the most perfect régime imaginable.

How easy it is to understand them!

They thought that they would be part of this new régime. And they followed Our Lord partly out of love and admiration and a desire for perfection and holiness, attracted by the splendour of His virtues, and partly in the thought of the solid temporal things which were going to come to them.

And then, suddenly, all is lost, ruined and destroyed.

And as an extra refinement to their misery, they must have been saying to themselves, as they went along the road, "When we get back home to the country, everyone will be able to make as much fun as they like of us, as dolts and boobies." All the sitters on the fence, all the clever people who preferred to wait and see, would be able to point at them. They would be able to sneer at the hotheads who went off just like that, without thinking, to follow an adventurer.

A WONDERFUL CONVERSATION

And as they go along with all this despair and bitterness in their hearts, and yet with something unforgettable still remaining in them from their contact with Our Lord, a traveller overtakes them in the evening and falls in beside them.

You know that wonderful conversation which we read at Mass on Easter Monday. "Why are you sad?" And they say, "You're the only man in all this district who doesn't know why all the people are sad. We had such hopes!" And they pour out all their hearts and tell him all that had happened and how it ended.

Then the traveller, beginning with Moses and the prophets,

shows them how it had been foretold; how it was necessary that the Messiah, having become man to ransom the sins of men, must Himself suffer even to death, in sacrifice, for the fault which was of infinite gravity because it offends against the Infinite. Wretched man is capable of an act of infinite evil, because evil—the gravity of the offence—is measured not by the greatness of him from whom it comes but by the greatness of him against whom it is committed. But when it comes to reparation, given that reparation is measured not by the measure of him who receives it but by the quality of him who offers it, man, who was capable of infinite evil, is incapable of performing a proportionate good in reparation.

Our Lord explains all this to them; the mystery of the Incarnation, which requires that it shall be the Infinite Himself who comes and offers reparation to the Infinite, so that there shall be a due proportion and that redemption shall be accomplished. But He had to become man Himself, not only to touch our hearts and to induce us to share in the redemption in communion with Him, but also in order that He should be able to offer reparation truly in the name of man.

THE MYSTERY OF THE SON OF MAN

This is the whole mystery of the Son of Man—that astonishing, overwhelming title. To think that, during all His years amongst us, the Eternal wished to be known only by this name and no other: the Son of Man. He, who is light and perfection and love and infinite energy; He who set the stars upon their course through space, who gave strength to the sun and a miraculous subtlety and delicacy of beauty to all the infinitely little things which we find throughout the world: He wished to have only this one title during those years: Son of Man.

He wanted us to understand the point to which He had identified Himself with our distress. He explains all this.

And now they have walked as far as the inn at Emmaus, a little village on the outskirts of Jerusalem. And the traveller makes as though to go on, while they go in to rest. And then they say that lovely thing, that phrase which we have decided to write up on the plain wall which is the only monument in the vault where our comrades of the Emmaus communities are buried: "Stay with us, Lord, because it is towards evening, and the day is now far spent."

And the traveller goes into the inn with them.

It has been evening twilight all this time. They haven't seen each other very well. Then, as they sit down to table, he takes the bread, breaks it, and gives it to them. Was it a eucharistic consecration? Perhaps. We do not know, and it does not matter. What we know is that at that moment they recognise Him and He disappears from their view.

Then the Gospel says: "And they said one to the other: Was not our heart burning within us, whilst He spoke in the way?"

This is something so profound and so powerful.

What this sentence of the Gospel seems to say, what these two men seem to give us as the most certain of all signs that they have not, in what they have seen with their eyes and received with their hands, been deceived by a mere appearance—the thing which is, for them, the most certain and decisive proof of all, is what they experienced within themselves: "Was not our heart burning within us, whilst He spoke in the way?"

And at once, these fugitives of a moment before, these

terror-stricken deserters, who had no courage left and no heart
for adventures any more, who had had only one idea—to get
back into the country—the Gospel tells us that straight away,
there and then, that night, they went back the way they had
come, utterly fearless, rushing back through the night to the
capital. They go straight to the place, the headquarters,
where they think they are likely to find the apostles, their
leaders. What leaders! Leaders in confusion, leaders who had
betrayed everything, who had fled in terror! But they think
that they are likely to find them gathered together in the place
where they lived with Our Lord.

And they think, no doubt, even more, that they are likely
to find Our Lady there. She is the only person of whom we
can think that, if faith did not disappear entirely from the
earth during those hours between the Passion of Our Lord
and the first appearances of the Resurrection, it was simply
because she was there, keeping it in her heart. Perhaps, during that Holy Saturday, the heart of the Virgin Mary was
the only human heart in which faith remained.

And now these two men who have seen the Lord, arrive at
the cenacle and come in shouting, "The Lord is alive!"

THE NEW ADVENTURE

A whole new world is opening before them. Death has been
defeated. The whole of mankind is rising again in Christ who
has risen again. Then they hear the apostles gathered there,
who have also recovered their morale, saying, "We know!
Peter and John saw the tomb empty this morning, and just
now, a few moments ago, the doors were shut and He came
in amongst us and ate with us."

And it was then, in reality, that the new adventure began. That miraculous adventure which goes on its way despite all our stumblings and darkness and sins and betrayals, down all the centuries and throughout the whole of man's world. The miraculous adventure of the message which passes on from one to another like a flame passing from one candle to another. The tremendous adventure of the message of God's love; God who loved men so much that He came and made Himself one of them, content to suffer from their cruelty, to suffer for them even to death, and, having died for them, to rise again and be amongst them again, staying with them in the tabernacle until the consummation—until His work should be completed, and all the human beings whom He willed to exist should have been able to know Him through the ministry and the apostolate of those to whom, in every age, He would have entrusted the responsibility of making Him known.

There had to be a disillusionment. Those men were generous, but at the same time they were living in an illusion. We must see this and understand it. This too is one of the fundamental aspects of the message we have received and which we are to pass on to the world.

The *wholeness* of man, in every order and domain of his being, lies in disillusionment; not disappointment and cynicism and believing in nothing, but believing in the truth and, day after day, clarifying our vision and going out of our illusions so as to attain to knowledge and to identify ourselves with reality, with the Eternal Being, God, who is love. This fundamental disillusionment is, at the same time, immeasurable hope. The certainty of total disillusionment is our sole and most abundant hope: the certainty that there will be an end to the world, and an end to our own lives—which are

illusions to each of us—the certainty that we shall enter into
that true and full life in which it will no longer be possible to
fail, in which it will no longer be possible to be a sinner, in
which it will no longer be possible to do anything evil; in
which it will be possible to bring to realisation the whole of
what our hearts are always in anguish for, even when we are
sinners.

You know the magnificent line from St. Augustine—that
worldly, artistic, intellectual, rich pagan. Disillusionment
pierced him, and he discovered reality. "Thou hast made us
for thyself, O God, and our hearts are restless till they rest in
thee."

Let us try to understand that the *wholeness* of our lives is
contained in what, in our Emmaus community, we like to call
enthusiastic disillusionment; disillusionment—a gradual getting clear from illusions—but a disillusionment which is
enthusiastic, in the proper sense of the word, which is "being
one with God."

Enthusiasm does not mean being an eccentric fanatic going
about with disordered hair and wild gestures. Enthusiasm is
the power of a person who is *one* with God. That is the strict,
primary meaning of the word. Enthusiastic disillusionment
means the wholeness of a man. It is the wholeness of a man in
business; he must quit his illusions if he is to do any good,
and know exactly what is useful and how it ought to be mar-
keted. It is the wholeness of a man who desires knowledge in
the order of science or art, so that he may go out of appearances and attain to the mystery of reality. And there must be
disillusionment at the level of the spiritual life, at the simplest
and most profound level of the mystical life, so as to attain,
beyond all that is illusory, to the intimate knowledge of God—
God who is love.

You see, we must never forget that we are in the most total

illusion of all, the most opaque and the most destructive of illusions, both within us and around us, so long as we do not love. And the greater the extent to which we are practising Catholics, if we do not love, the more serious and dangerous and sure to damn us that illusion is.

What we must understand is that for God only one thing is the *end,* and that is Himself, because that alone exists infinitely and eternally. Now He Himself is love, and the only thing which can concern Him when He creates free, reasonable, responsible beings is that these beings, with their freedom, should achieve love. God can have no other end than that which is, which means that eternal love which He Himself is. And all the other things are only means, ways which He puts at our disposal so as to make it possible for us to advance all together, as a community, mutually helping each other, towards that love.

Let us hold on to this and never forget it.

RECOURSE TO OUR LADY

May this time of Lent—this time of waiting and tension in preparation for the sovereign disillusionment of the Resurrection at Easter—be filled with our prayers to Our Lord that we may offer ourselves to disillusionment, which means to the encounter with Him. Let us ask Mary, who, like every true mother, is forever waiting—

Mary who is the mother of all holiness, the mother of the community of the Church, and through the community of the Church the mother of all humanity, which Our Lord entrusted to her on the Cross;

Mary, daughter of Israel, who lived in the expectation of

the Messiah, in an expectation which was so great that the
Lord had already chosen her to be the mother who would
give us the Child Jesus;

Mary who, while her Child grew, lived, like every mother,
waiting for what was to be the destiny of her Child, waiting
daily in constant tension and anguish and pain;

Mary who, by her Assumption, is now body and soul in
heaven;

Mary who lives now in expectation of the end, expectation
of the completion and fulfilment of the world, which is the
creation of her Son, the Eternal Word;

Mary the mother who, each day and always, brings to
birth not only the life of her Child but every moment in the
life of that Child, bearing Him within her, suffering when He
suffers, suffering with us when we are sinners, when we grow
shabby and mediocre;

Mary who, in this sanctuary, has for centuries granted so
many graces, so much help and so much comfort—even more
than material help; let us ask her from the bottom of our
hearts really to take us in hand, to scold us every evening for
not having loved enough during the day. May she, throughout
the entire world, multiply in the hearts of men and women,
and especially of young people, a restless longing to give themselves and to love, so that there may be a hundredfold increase
in these new vocations to be missionaries of distress and poverty. May they increase in such measure as to fill the immensity
of the need, these vocations to boys and girls to give themselves, for a part of their life or the whole of it, to their
suffering brothers, giving themselves to them to share their
conditions, not to give them help from outside but to become
incarnate in the midst of them, so as to put into practice what
Our Lord put into practice and what He wants us to put into

practice with Him: redemption through incarnation, the salvation of all through self-identification with all, suffering with those who suffer, weeping with those who weep, so that the day may come when no one weeps any longer, because together we have found the way of the Lord.

Let us ask Our Lady for this.

If we really ask her, and if we do our best each day, she will grant it, and she will help us to see, to realise, that to do the work of God it is not necessary to start by becoming quite free from all failings. It is enough that we should live, with all our strength, in the tension of hope, in Our Lord's hands, so as to come, with Him, to love enough to be able to recognise and serve Him first of all in those of our brothers who are suffering the most. Amen.

AT THE FACULTY OF MEDICINE, PARIS*

At the Last Judgment, there will be no more lies, no more playacting, no more conventions, no more distinctions of rank or education; all there will be is a plain revelation of love and hate. And hate is not only, nor primarily, a matter of angry shouting or of evildoing; it lies primarily in the passive indifference with which people who have too much to eat and live in too great comfort go on being a glaring insult to those who are unfortunate.

We must be frank about this. It is true that the class war is a mistake. But what we must not ignore is that there are two aspects to the class war. There is the one aspect, of individuals and groups submitting to stricter and stricter organization and boasting, in rebellious anger, that they are going to smash everything to pieces. True enough. But we must be clearsighted enough to realise that this is only the second stage in the class war. There is another, without which this second aspect would never have existed. That other is the class war which all of us, you and I—I, at any rate—have carried on at some time or other by being passively indifferent in the presence of people suffering even unto death.

---

* Professor Richet in the Chair 10th of June, 1955.

148

That is the truth. And we must keep on saying this truth, tirelessly, with all the passion of true love, which begins in a hunger and thirst for justice. No excuse is needed for putting passion into our denunciation of what is the shame and dishonour, and at last the death, of any nation.

They tell us lies. We are told lies every day by those official voices whose sounding-board is the press. They give us figures, but they are always absolute figures, never comparative ones; they never make any comparison between achievements and needs. So, they say, we have provided 100,000, 135,000, 175,000 new homes . . . it's going up . . . wonderful, isn't it? What they don't say is that by providing these 160,000 or 170,000 homes for the population of France during 1954 we not only have not improved the housing situation, but we have not even maintained the level of the previous year. Taking into account the increase in marriages, changes in the population and depreciation of houses which have become unsanitary or dangerous, we should need almost 200,000 a year simply to keep abreast of the situation. With 200,000 new homes a year we should *begin* to gain ground. By so much as we fall short of that figure, that is the number of families which we are in practice adding each year to the mass of families already homeless.

That is the truth, and that is our shame.

Tens of thousands of working-class families hear it said, and said again, that there is no money available for the H.L.M., that there just isn't enough, there's no money available for loans for house purchase; but there is money available this week to manufacture artificial snow in the month of June at the Porte Maillot—snow, they proudly tell us, which will

actually fall on the audience itself, as a final touch to the
pleasures of high society. When a community has got to this
point, it is ripe for destruction.

I am not against sport; I know how important it is, and I
am sure we shall never have enough sport or enough stadiums.
We can never have enough ways of making people healthy.
Nor am I against attracting tourists; there are heaps of people
who have to live that way. But there are minimum standards
of decency which ought to be respected. When a country like
France cannot provide enough homes to save her children
from dying, we can only declare that politicians who put on
spectacles of this sort are not statesmen but imbecile *agents
provocateurs* engaged in fomenting rebellion.

Try for a moment to put yourselves in the place of our
families living in the fields at Noisy-le-Grand. This is where
we bought twenty acres of land last year so as to have somewhere to put families in rather less desperate conditions than
those at the camp at Pomponne. We did it on the day when
they threw us out of the entrances to the Métro and closed
them, one after the other, and then threw us out of our camp
at the Porte de Vanves, where, you may remember, we put up
some tents one night at two o'clock in the morning, in defiance
of the authorities, so that next day the authorities found themselves confronted by a population of nine hundred people
taking shelter there. Try to put yourselves in the place of those
hundreds of families, still sleeping in tents, with their children.
Think of the rage and fury you would feel.

I do not know whether all the families living there are
legitimate; but I do know that when children are born, any
nation which is not simply savage has the responsibility of
providing them with conditions worthy of human beings, from
the moment they begin to exist.

You may say, truly enough, that amongst them all there are some cases of undesirable people. There certainly are a few cases, in every two hundred, of what you might call undesirables; but find me any group of two hundred families, in the most select district you like, which won't include a few undesirables! I don't want to imply that the world of the poor is *better* than the upper-class world, but it is not true that it is worse. It's all the same humanity, with the same vices and virtues, mothers struggling in the same way to bring up their children; they are exactly the same, with the same wish to do right, only they have more excuse when they fail because they simply cannot cope.

Now, listen to this. We have more than two hundred families up there, living in the little forty-square-yard huts that we've built for about two hundred thousand francs each: they have one big living room where the father and mother sleep, and a little room for the boys and another for the girls. For them, that's paradise. They were living in a tent until December. It wasn't till February or March that we were able to take down all the tents, and everyone was really housed in a little place of their own.

Now, when spring came, the pressure of homeless families begging us for help was such that when I came back after my long illness, a month and a half ago, my friends said to me, "Father, you forbade us to put up any more tents this winter, but look! Out of the twenty families who came today, there's this man who just can't go on; his wife is at the end of her tether; there are fifteen of them in one room. She wants to throw herself into the Seine. And then, this man has already tried to kill his children," etc.

So they begged me, at Noisy-le-Grand, to buy tents at about twenty thousand francs for desperate families like these and put them up there. Faced with people sleeping out of doors, how could I refuse? I said yes, after all.

But realising that the repercussions from this would be protests from the authorities—for whom poverty is endurable just so far as it remains out of sight—we drew up a form letter to be sent to the Prefect each time a family who were in the street, and didn't know where to go, came and begged us for a tent, and we consented.

It is for each man to shoulder his own responsibilities, or to resign his public functions if the law does not allow him to carry them out humanely.

The solution certainly is *not* to have everyone scavenging in dustbins, or Cabinet Ministers sleeping in the streets, but to have everyone, according to his own duty, his own responsibility, his own social level and function and position, doing what depends on him; doing what he can and should do to ensure that those who are suffering most shall be served first. We ought to be able to look one another in the face and say that much. And if we are to achieve it, we must have *some* people going to extremes of love, not only deciding to serve first those who are suffering most, but deciding to share their conditions. In the matter of human suffering, in an age like that in which we are living, there are no merely national problems. From henceforth, all these problems are closely linked at the international, world-wide level.

Thou shalt love thy "neighbour." The word "neighbour" is a wonderfully accurate and extraordinarily large word. It is a much more beautiful and absolute word than "others." It takes God to find terms of such strength and precision as this! When God says, "Thou shalt love thy neighbour," it implies both order and infinity, both a priority and an absence of limitations. It means "Begin by loving whoever is nearest to you." And then go on to infinity, from nearest to nearest, so that your love does not stop till it has reached the ends of the earth. This is our duty: both to love our nearest neighbour and then, once we have made sure that he has what he needs, to love as much as we can, with all our strength, to the measure of the whole world.

To consider our nearest neighbours first: it needs to be said that in this country, where we have the housing problem in so tragic and scandalous a form, the time has come, especially after the events of eighteen months ago, when we can no longer put up with the sort of—I don't know what word to use for it—the sort of trickery and frivolity which is going on. I mean the attempt, after the tremendous wave which swept up from the whole nation last year, to make out in some way that housing the people of France is a problem for welfare organisations; that the Abbé Pierre and those "splendid" rag-pickers of his (they are sometimes "splendid" and sometimes "dreadful," according to the needs of the case) and a few other welfare organisations are quite enough, on their own, to solve at least the urgent problems.

We have had enough of this absurdity! The rising last year certainly *was* a wave of generous kindness, let no one make any mistake about that. There certainly was kindness in it, limitless kindness, far beyond what anyone could have imagined. But, as I have said so often and am determined to shout again and again, there was something in it altogether different from a simple upsurge of kindness. And woe to those who saw in it or wished others to see in it only a wave of sentiment! First and foremost it was the protest of a whole people, which knows that it is not a nation of fools and has had enough

of seeing itself governed as if it were a nation of fools. The
nation had understood that it is not merely cruel and wicked
but, first and foremost, *absurd* to let children die and families
be sunk in degradation.

What happened last year was primarily a sort of uprising
and explosion of consciences protesting against an absurdity.

There is no doubt about it. And there isn't a sensible, honest
man who could force himself to endure all this pretty-pretty,
sentimental, adulatory literature which is stuffing us with a
picture of that "holy man" the Abbé Pierre, after a dose of
which one sheds a tear over some photograph and goes home
convinced that, having shed it, one's duty is done. Of such
admiration, I will only say—keep it to yourselves, I'm fed to
the teeth with it.

What we need is something else. It's not a matter of kindness, or "charity," or sentimentality or admiration, it is a matter of justice, and such vital justice that, if it is not satisfied,
it will become the duty of love itself to grow angry, and to
accomplish by force of anger what could not be accomplished
by force of peace. It is no longer to be endured.

Let's be serious. Supposing that the horror of another war
broke over us tomorrow, and that the circumstances were such
that opinion was undivided, that the whole nation was unanimous in saying, "We must go to it and defend ourselves."
What should we see? Within twenty-four hours we should find
the financial resources, the materials, the machines, the labour
force, the experts needed to manufacture arms for defending
our liberty and all the good things which we believe are contained in it. And we should be right to defend what we hold
to be sacred and what we think of as life itself.

But why then, with the war over, when it is not a question
of defending liberty but of the lives, the bodies and souls, the

health and the future of the children of France—how does it happen that all those in responsible positions tell us: "It isn't possible, it's insoluble. We should need ten, twenty, thirty years. We haven't the machines, we haven't the money, we haven't the trained people, we haven't the materials, we can't do it. . . ."

It's beyond me. And I think the time has come to say to our government, "Stop this tragic mockery."

When the war is over and it is simply a question of a peace-time crisis, the problem arises from the fact that those on whom the decisions depend know perfectly well that there is no possibility that *their* wives and children will have to sleep in the street tomorrow. So, since they no longer feel personally threatened, since they no longer feel that they personally are in danger, they lose their creative imagination and become incapable of inventing or applying bold, sweeping, rapid solutions which would supply a remedy and save the people.

Every time we go short of a thousand million for building, it is, for practical purposes, as though we agreed to vote four, five or ten thousand million in future years for looking after delinquents, abandoned children, prostitutes, alcoholics, mad-men and criminals. What we refuse for building we have to grant for police, judges, courts, hospitals, sanatoriums and prisons.

We need to be aware of this. It is not true that these credits are refused because of economic and financial difficulties.

We must understand that a problem of this gravity, both material and moral, is not going to be solved by the State alone. Nor is it going to be solved by private enterprise on its own, even if we have the wisest possible legislation, as favourable as it can be to the investment of private capital in building.

Faced with a problem of this magnitude, either we are not

really in earnest—and those who believe that France is finished are right—or else we must realise that there is no solution short of *a real mobilisation of the whole nation for building.*

Faced with flood, earthquake, war or any full-sized crisis, the nation has to be mobilised: a summons has to go out to the whole soul of the people and to all its material resources.

But what use is the State, once peace is restored, if it is not capable of using, in the service of life, all the devices which it used during the time of bloodshed?

The truth is that all the means are there, and such was the great lesson of last winter. And, for a start, the first and most necessary and most irreplaceable of those means is not lacking to us: We have it in superabundance.

Outside France, and often inside France too, people say and repeat and suggest that the youth of France has gone to pieces; that it spends its time decadently in cafés, that it is good for nothing, that it is incapable of having ideals or enthusiasm or energy. It is an infamous and stupid lie. For the greatest lesson of last winter was the overwhelming proof it gave that, when the people of France is invited to sacrifice itself for something worth while, it is as capable of doing so today as it was yesterday or at any other period. And if it doesn't, it is because there is no one able to appeal to it and inspire confidence in it.

What we must consecrate ourselves to today is the mobilisation of the youth of France. All the speeches about upsurges of generous kindness and so on are over and done with.

The thing before us now, of which everyone needs to be aware, is that we are going to struggle by every means open to us until we have some kind of government capable of mobilising the nation to save the country in the housing crisis.

Two days ago I was in the office of one of the highest officials in Paris. I do not often have occasion to say this, but I am saying it now, loud and clear: I had the feeling that day that here was someone who was not only a very high official but at the same time a man with a large and really human heart.

As I said good-bye to him I said: "This is what I am resolved to do. . . . Now, I know that quite often people are going to say that it is illegal and irregular. What I am asking you to do, then, is to repeat what I am resolved to repeat, tirelessly, as I have for so long already: Is this, or is it not, necessary if homes and children's lives are to be saved? If it is not necessary, prove it: I only ask to be convinced; show me another solution. But if it is necessary, then recognise the fact that it is your law which is illegal because it is inhuman."

If what is necessary does not fit in with the law, then it is the law which is wrong and which has to be changed.

Children are not to die to please the people who make the laws; it is the law which must be changed, so that children can live without their lives being illegal.

I do not think I am saying anything excessive, though I realise that it is something rather appalling, when I say that a government which, in face of the gravity of the present housing crisis in France, does not prove itself capable of such a national mobilisation, ought to be considered, in the name of the natural law and the law of God, an illegitimate government. For it has been put into power in order to house its people.

If we do not get two hundred thousand million francs out of Parliament for building houses for rent under H.L.M., this is what we must say to Parliament, and keep on saying; this is what you must keep writing to your deputies, so as to give them no peace: "You are scoundrels; you may be doing it

unconsciously, but you are scoundrels, because you are in fact
betraying the trust which has been placed in you. If you cannot do it out of pity or a sense of duty, at least do it out of
common sense." But are they capable of having this kind of
practical common sense, the only kind which is of use in
politics, and which is only to be had by living in close contact
with those who suffer? Do you think that the privileges of
privileged people can go on indefinitely? When we are told
that there are fifty thousand unoccupied rooms in Paris, according to the lists of the public authorities (and in this field
it is not possible to accuse the public authorities of dema-
goguery!), that there are three thousand of them in this
arrondissement alone, do you believe that this is a state of
affairs which can go on indefinitely?

I am going to end by telling you a story which I think quite
delicious.

Some little time ago, in a district which I will not name,
we organised a squatters' invasion, adding one more to that
tale of crimes with which we have been gaily loading our
consciences for many months. We made very careful prepara-
tions, the doors opened as though by magic, and we thus
housed twelve families: sixty people, of whom thirty-one were
children. The owner, an admirable man, came to see me, but
I had left for America. When I arrived in New York I had
a telephone call from a gentleman of considerable position
who asked me to meet him. When we had met he explained
that he was a friend of the owner of this property. The latter
had twice telephoned him from Paris, begging him to appeal
to me—to appeal to my better feelings and ask me to order
those twelve families to move out of his premises.

I was in New York. I did not quite see myself sending

imperative orders to those twelve families to move out of the house with their children the day they got my telegram. I explained to this gentleman that it would be difficult for me to turn those people out. I said that there was only one way to go about it: seeing that the owner was such an important person, with such important connections, and that we, on the other hand, had some little prefabricated houses which could be erected very quickly, he should approach the administration of the municipality of Paris to authorise us to put them up on some unoccupied site; and then he, this very rich man in New York, should approach his friends so as to collect the necessary funds for us to build these twelve houses for the twelve families, an undertaking for which we would provide free labour. . . .

And then came this delicious touch. Quite spontaneously and straightforwardly and frankly this gentleman said to me: "But, monsieur l'Abbé, do you realise what you are saying? It's blackmail! *Just because the Government has not done its duty and there are not enough houses in France, why does it have to be my friend who suffers the consequences?*"

"Oh my dear sir," I answered, "how happy you are making me! What hopes are opening before us now! If the fact that the Government has not done its duty is beginning at last to have unpleasant consequences for the people who *are* well housed, there may begin to be a real chance that the Government, whose ear they have because it belongs to their comfortable world, may begin to bestir itself. Have you ever considered," I said, making myself clear, "that the day when our squatters moved into your friend's house was not the day when the Government began failing to 'do its duty,' as you say. But so long as that failure did not affect *you*, you saw no great harm in it; so long as it was only these others, these children,

who suffered from it. What hopes we may have, if the scandal
has grown so enormous that it begins to overflow onto the
people who *are* well housed, and to produce some appreciable
inconveniences for them. Really, what you say is wonderfully
encouraging.

"You can count on us not to forget the lesson. You may be
sure that we shall repeat the offence over and over again; that
we shall pile up as many troubles as possible for the people
who have been, till now, 'out of it,' and have therefore been
so patient over the sufferings of others. You have become our
most precious allies. We shall do all that is necessary to ensure
that so powerful a reinforcement is never lacking to us, regard-
less of the cost . . . to you!"

We are going to show a film which was taken in this district.
Look at it and let it work on you. Think of your children, and
of yourselves when you were children.

The secret of achieving understanding in social and political
matters, the one necessary condition, is to put yourself in the
other person's place.

Try to do this, even if it means depriving yourself of some
extra, even if it means depriving your children of some extra
which you would have liked to offer them. Tell them why.
And think of this: by depriving your children of some luxury
and explaining why, you will have given them, at a deeper
level, something much more than the present you would like
to have given them, for you will have taught them the mystery
of joy which is contained in true love.

What better or more real thing can a father and mother
give their children as they grow up than love—real love, not
a sterile sentiment, but that devouring love which begins in a
hunger and thirst for justice? Remember that if you give your

children that, by drawing them in to the sacrifice you make in giving to those who are now coming amongst you to ask for subscriptions to help house a hundred families in this district, you will deserve to feel that your home is not accursed; that there does not rest upon it that curse which rests upon the homes of those who remain indifferent to the excessive suffering in the homes of others. Real blasphemy does not consist in the angry cries of a man who is afflicted with an excess of suffering. Real blasphemy consists in the indifference of those who remain unaffected by the profanation of the image of God which is taking place in so many human beings all around us.

MEETING IN THE SALLE PLEYEL*

First of all, my friends, I want to thank you from the very bottom of my heart for having come here in such crowds. It is such an encouragement.

This is something I have said many times over recently— too much, it may have seemed, but not really.

ADMIRATION IS STERILE, FRIENDSHIP FERTILE

Eighteen months ago something fantastic and unforeseeable occurred, and a work in which we had been engaged for years, trying, in company with a few friends, to give ourselves as well as we could, suddenly became famous. Since then some of us, and myself in particular, have found ourselves the centre of a sort of universal admiration which is becoming intolerable. Believe me when I tell you, from the bottom of my heart, that if I have ever during my life had any temptations to vanity I have been well punished for them; for experience has proved that, though a little admiration is not unpleasant, beyond a certain point it becomes unbearable.

I am saying this quite simply, as a man talking to men.

---

* 16th of June 1955.

162

Give us friendship, a practical, active, intelligent friendship prepared to exchange ideas with us—because we haven't any ready-made solutions, we are no cleverer than anyone else—a friendship in which we can act on these problems confronting us, which have aroused your consciences as human beings: all these complex, innumerable problems of human distress and despair.

Do not give us admiration, for admiration is usually sterile; give us friendship, which is active, intelligent and militant.

Don't be like those people who shed tears of admiration over a photograph of the Abbé Pierre and think that they have thus fulfilled their duty. It is nothing like enough, and they are liable to find that we are not at all grateful to them.

A BOLD DECISION

We have met this evening to discuss a clearly defined subject. You have seen the title of this lecture: "America 1955: Danger and Hope for the World."

The decision to give this lecture was taken absolutely on the spur of the moment. When I came back from the United States, newspaper men began to come and pester me. I told them that I couldn't possibly see them one after the other, so I invited them to come all together. Well, when I had finished my interview with those thirty or forty journalists, they were still putting so many questions, and there were still so many subjects which needed to be talked about, that this idea was put forward : why not have a public meeting where you could say these things not simply to newspaper men but directly to all the people—to anyone who cared to come. So we took the risk—one more crazy thing to add to our record! We took the risk of booking the Salle Pleyel, and, though the cost might be high, we considered whether or not we ought to make people pay to come in. We decided not, because it had to be possible for everyone to come. Really, we did not know whether there would be anyone interested in the subject. And here you are, so now it is for me to speak to you.

WHY GO TO AMERICA?

What was that journey of mine?

How did it come to be planned?

Eight or ten months ago, various friends of ours who live in the United States—the most eminent being our dear friend that great Frenchman Jacques Maritain, who has now been living for years in the middle of America's youth, teaching in the University of Princeton—wrote to say that they hoped I would come and speak especially to the youth of America.

You know how I was ill for many months. When I was convalescent and came back to Paris, it was almost the date which had been fixed for this journey. Should I go, or should we cancel it?

For a moment we thought of cancelling the trip, because it seemed so necessary that I should be here, to take up the work with my friends again after those five months of illness. But it was those friends themselves—the committees and communities of ragpickers and builders—who said, "Father, you must go. We want you to; we shall have to get on without you for another month, that can't be helped. You must go and tell those fellows what we would tell them if we could go ourselves."

And when I was over there, I often said: I have been a

Member of Parliament for a long time, but I have never in my life had such a sense of truly being a deputy as I did during this journey. For I was deeply conscious that it was my responsibility to say the things which are weighing on the souls and hearts of those in our country who are suffering most, and, through and beyond them, to some extent of those who are suffering most through the human race.

So the trip was decided upon. It consisted of three weeks in the United States, a few days making contacts at the United Nations headquarters, and a few days at the end in Canada, added on at the last moment.

Obviously, it would be absolutely ridiculous to pretend I could give you a sort of complete and penetrating analysis of the state of America, in all its vastness, after three weeks spent in visiting five cities in the United States. I went to New York, Washington, Chicago, Los Angeles, and San Francisco. Then I went back to New York for these contacts at the United Nations, and then on to Montreal. So, geographically speaking, my contact with the country was very scattered, very unmethodical, very narrow, and much too short to tell me everything about it.

All the same, it was extremely instructive and valuable despite its brevity.

SEEKING TO KNOW HUMAN BEINGS

I was not trying to study American power, or American technique, or American internal or international politics. What I was concerned with, what I wanted to focus all my attention upon, was to get to know and understand America not as a reservoir of material power but as a reservoir of human beings—one of the greatest reservoirs of human beings in the world today.

I know—because someone telephoned a few minutes ago to tell me—that there are in this audience—and I want to thank them, gladly, and as a free man—representatives of the diplomatic corps from some of the embassies which are most opposed to each other. I rejoice with all my heart, because this makes me feel absolutely free in what I am going to say.

So, then, I tried to understand the human quality of the vast reserve of humanity represented by that great power.

What method did I use to make the soul of that people vibrate so as to try to hear what kind of sound might be drawn from it? It was a simple method, so simple that it seemed eccentric; for simple things have grown so rare that using them gives people a surprise.

This was my method. From the first sentence I said in public, when the tugs came to take the *Ile-de-France* in tow and the newspaper men came on board and began hurling questions at me, I said: "It's perfectly clear. I am a Frenchman, and I have not come to talk about France. I am a priest, and I have not come to talk about the Church. I am a former Member of Parliament, and I have not come to talk about politics. And I have come to America, and I have not come to talk about America. So what have I come to do? I have simply come as a man to talk to other men of good will about the overwhelming problems facing man today throughout the whole world."

NO MONEY, THANK YOU

I then added, "Now, don't faint: I've come from Europe, and I haven't come to ask for money." They said at once,

"This is incredible! No one has come from Europe since the war for anything except to ask for money."

But I went on to say, "Look out! It's something much worse. If I haven't come to ask for money, I've come to ask for much more. I've come to tell you that what the world needs you to give it, is something quite other than your money."

And that was my theme in all the meetings.

How were the meetings held?

There was one big meeting in every town, and sometimes as many as four. At City Hall, New York, there were 1,235 people (they have statistics perfectly taped over there, so they gave me the exact entrance figure!). And I didn't speak English. I began with a couple of sentences saying, "I was a bad pupil at school, and you will have to bear the consequences, because I won't be able to speak your language. So, please be indulgent." I would say a few words, and an interpreter translated them. We held all the meetings in this uncomfortable fashion, with an interpreter, and yet everywhere there were crowds as big as you are tonight.

Besides these public meetings, which always ended with long conversations with people who pressed round me at the end of the meeting, we had a large number of small meetings, with groups of twenty, forty or fifty people: interracial groups, interdenominational groups, social action groups, all sorts.

In the committee which sponsored the trip, under the presidency of Jacques Maritain, there were as many Protestants as Catholics; there were Jews, Quakers, and all the social organisations in the country.

Finally, we had a relatively large number of individual conversations, as many as could be arranged, both with outstanding personalities—members of the hierarchies of all the religious, political, trade union and university bodies—and

with ordinary citizens, humble apostles working in the service
of poverty. For, I assure you, it exists over there too!

What exactly was it that I asked them to look at, at all
these meetings?

I am going to consider it this evening under three headings:

1. I will tell you exactly what I said to them.
2. How they reacted to my theme, what their response was.
3. What conclusions I have drawn relative to our hopes
and fears for the future, and finally what are our own responsibilities. For it is not enough to measure with an Olympian
eye the responsibilities, merits and faults of others; there is
nothing valuable in such considerations unless they end by an
examination of one's own conscience and a realisation of how
one needs to act in the light of what one has observed.

1. WHAT DID I TELL THEM?

This is quite simple. I said to them:

The great crisis in the world today is just this: more than
a thousand million human beings are living in conditions
worse than those of animals. Three quarters of the people in
the world today do not eat the minimum necessary to grow
into adults. One out of every two families, every two human
couples in the world today, has no home.

Now, the world is becoming aware of these facts, and is
trying to make effective efforts to grapple with them, some
because of their consciences and a sense of duty and others—
even if they have no sense of duty—because of a sense of
necessity and desire for safety.

They are always telling us about these two blocks whose

mutual antagonism constitutes the chief threat to the world and to the future, but, as a way of expressing the world situation, this is an absolute sham. It is the third block which is going to be the master of the world of the future: the thousand million human beings who have no roof over their heads or bread to eat or schools or hospitals. What will decide the future of the world is onto which side they cast their hopes.

Without any exaggeration, with all strict, scientific accuracy, we may say that it is that fraction of humanity which is living in subhuman poverty which is going to be the arbiter of history.

It is poverty which shall judge the world.

Now, faced with these two facts—the fact of poverty itself, and the fact that poverty will decide the issues of tomorrow, great efforts are being made.

And this is the genesis of the great crisis in the world.

GOOD WILL HELD IN CHECK

Any well-informed, honest and clearheaded person must recognise that all the very considerable—though quite insufficient—efforts which have been made, in materials, money, technical aid, and good will have produced results which are merely ridiculous. There is a great deal of good will in the world, more perhaps than there has ever been before. When people say to me, "Abbé, you know politicians, you can tell us the truth—they're all scoundrels, aren't they?" I always say, "It's not true! There are some dishonest men amongst them, but no more than there are among the electors."

When we look at the extent of the sacrifices which have been accepted, and then at the results obtained, we cannot but observe that these results have been absolutely infinitesimal; and moreover, in several cases already, they have been not only infinitesimal but actually the direct opposite of what had been hoped for. We observe that the loans and economic aid given to several countries in the world have not only been ineffectual but have simply accelerated the process of corruption, degradation, anarchy and despair, and, in the end, the surrender of these peoples to tyranny and dictatorship or some kind of desperate solution. There are thus many cases where efforts made with good will have only accelerated the disintegration of what they were meant to save.

REASONS FOR THIS HELPLESSNESS

Proceeding with my analysis of the situation, I said to my American audiences: How are we to explain that power is thus powerless, and techniques and skill and money all ineffective? We must discover the reasons.

Perhaps we can draw a lesson from my own experience: a small experience, minute if measured on the scale of world affairs, in which a few friends and myself found ourselves involved, and in which we witnessed comparatively large results being produced by absurdly small means; a sort of laboratory experiment, in which small means have produced big results, in contrast to the small results which have been produced by large-scale means.

What lesson can we learn from the Emmaus experiment?

This is how I tried to describe it to them. Look at society as it is—society inside each nation and society at the level of international relations.

Society is fated to be composed of two parts—first of all,

those who, in one way or another, dispose of some sort of power: political, financial, cultural, influential.

Now, those who hold the power, even if they are the best men in the world, are fated, by the very nature of the power they hold, to become very rapidly estranged from that real and tragic knowledge of the situation which is possessed by those who are in need. Even if they are very good men, they may have, statistically and scientifically, a perfect knowledge of all the different kinds of distress existing among their own people and throughout the world, but they have lost and cannot regain what we may call flesh-and-blood knowledge: the knowledge which a body has if it is its own hand which is crushed; the knowledge which a Minister of Reconstruction would have of the housing crisis if it were his own daughter who had to sleep in one room with fifteen other people tonight.

Now, I am not saying this as a reproach. It is almost an ontological observation: the exercise of power, by its very nature, separates a man from the knowledge of distress.

Distress, on the other hand, once it reaches a certain level of depth, becomes something which renders the man undergoing it incapable of struggling to save himself; incapable even of speaking to express his despair.

Consider the reality of this human distress in its depths.

Take the starving people in Bombay or Calcutta whom they pick up by cartloads every morning and throw into a common grave because they have died of hunger during the night. It is not thinkable that it should be they themselves who can effectively organise a movement of protest to demand a policy on a world-wide scale to supply them with food—food which does exist, since it proves quite possible to send it from one end of the world to the other in time of war, as supplies to armies. It is not possible that people who are suffering primitive, basic distress in such a degree as this should be able, by themselves, to obtain their rights in the matter of food, or even manage to proclaim their needs.

To take a form of distress nearer home: it isn't thinkable that a protest movement should be started on the initiative of the mothers who see their husbands come back, later each evening, to what you can't call a home; the one room where they and the children are all piled on top of each other, perhaps with another young family as well; a room where there isn't a corner to put a chair for a man to sit in after his work. Inevitably, such a man will go and pass his evenings in a bar, because he knows that if he comes back to this room he'll lose his temper, torment his wife and cuff the children. He is tired after his day's work. He goes out into the street, and, inevitably, to a bar.

Is it thinkable that we should have a protest movement organised by a mother who sees her husband going down hill every day, turning into an addict, an invalid, an alcoholic, without meaning to; a mother who has to put her children to sleep in her and her husband's bed, or—and this is not something dug out of a petrol-can shantytown in Algeria, but happens right in Paris itself—has to hang the chairs up on a nail on the wall so as to have somewhere to put the palliasses on the ground?

A few weeks ago a French bishop told me of something that happened in a family in his own episcopal city—not in a family of tramps or spendthrifts, but in the family of one of his Catholic Actionists. A death had occurred at the end of the day, and it was not possible to take the body out of the house because it was too late in the evening. The vigil went on through the night, and the children were drooping with exhaustion. The room was so small that they had to put those children, seven or eight years old, to bed on the same mattress on which the corpse was lying. That happened in our land of France. It would perhaps be impossible to find an "uncivilised" country in which people were reduced to such a level.

We must have the courage to look these things in the face, to let them really hurt us and make us look into ourselves and ask ourselves whether we have gone mad, whether we have turned cowardly and betrayed our duty, as human beings, to our brothers.

How can you expect mothers living in conditions like these, thousands of them—for there are ten thousand families in and around Paris living in conditions like these—to be able to organise a demonstration and come out in the streets with placards demanding redress? The blow has been dealt them at such a humiliating level, in such an intimate fibre of their being, that they are reduced to silence.

The tragedy of this world lies in its being divided between unseeing power and powerless knowledge.

THE PROPHET

The root of it lies in the absence of any connecting machinery between the power which doesn't know, which cannot know in the full tragic sense, and the tragedy which has no means of expressing itself.

And I explained to the Americans, the practical people who reckon everything in figures and dollars, what it is that we haven't got which could bridge this gulf between power and suffering. What we lack is a quite small matter. And if we are incapable of bringing it to life again, we shall have to consider that all that we love is lost, and cannot be defended by arms or material powers of any sort whatever. What matters is to know whether we shall be able to bring to life again this trifling thing, this foolish little thing, this infinitesimal little thing which is needed if we are to re-establish a dialogue in society and open a way for passion to enter once more into governmental circles.

What is it that is needed?

What is needed, and what we discovered in our little Emmaus experiment, is what I will call, by a similitude, the function of the prophet in the city.

What is needed is that there should be a few fools, just a small number, but that small number is indispensable, who deliberately decide to go, voluntarily, and share the lot of those who are suffering:

Not individually, for then they will either, having plunged into suffering, be overwhelmed by it and become unable to speak, or else, so as to retain their ability to speak, they will hold a little aloof from it and will have no authority to speak because they are not part of it. They must be right in the suffering, voluntarily sharing the lot of those who suffer.

And they must be in it as a group, so that the group will give them the strength to be right in and yet not be swept away by the torrent.

Finally, while sharing the lot of those who suffer, sharing it as a group so as to retain their effectiveness, they must be resolved to live in that suffering while keeping themselves with some work which will guarantee them absolute economic autonomy. It does not matter if it is the lowest sort of work there is—scavenging in dustbins and rubbish—but they must be able to stand up and say: I owe nothing to anybody and so I can speak, because I know suffering, I live with those who have to bear it; I am not overwhelmed by it, because the strength of the group saves me from that, and I can face the whole world as a free man because I owe my bread to nothing but my own work.

And to those neighbours of ours—once again, remember that they are calculating, practical, matter-of-fact men, men concerned with money—I explained all this in the fashion of a madman used to being considered as one crying in the wilderness: at bottom, what I am saying is that we must have a renewal of the function of the prophet in the city.

The prophet is *pro phemi*, which means he who speaks *for,* not he who speaks in advance, not he who makes predictions. In the prophets of Israel, for every ten lines of prediction there are a hundred pages which simply represent a man's voice saying to the prince: "Your power was given for defending and succouring those who suffer, not for heaping up more and more privileges for those who are already fortunate." That is what the prophet is.

And that is what has disappeared from the city today. It was a function of primitive monasticism; but the monastery, whose recent renewal of life has been so wonderful in so many ways, has stopped half way and failed to recover its social and sociological significance. Though including so much that is admirable, the monastic revival of the last hundred and fifty years has stopped half way, restoring something which does not connect with primitive monasticism because it has become something for the select few. A monastery no longer represents the voice of those who have no voice, nor is it any longer a presence in the midst of those who suffer.

And perhaps the question that matters is whether we shall prove capable of bringing this thing to life again in our society today.

A prophet cannot be elected, nor paid a salary, nor can he be a trade unionist, who is both paid a salary and elected by his comrades. We have to have members of Parliament, and trade unionists, and civil servants. But unless their work is preceded by the presence of a few slightly crazy people flinging themselves into the midst of distress in order to share in communion with the suffering of those they wish to save, then however gigantic the efforts made and however huge the amounts of financial and economic aid voted, all these efforts will be powerless and ineffectual, and will often actually have a corrupting influence.

Then as a final simplification—after which I shall have done with what I said to them—I used to end by saying this.

Don't you think that our world today has grown rather like a wonderful ultra-modern house, equipped with all the most superb devices and gadgets? The father of the house is an electrician, and a genius about all the most amazing modern techniques. Then one day, in their ultra-modern house with its technical genius living in it, the most wonderful machine of all, the colour television set, breaks down. Father takes off his coat, takes his box of tools and his spare parts, and sets to work. He spares neither trouble nor expense; time passes; and it still won't work. Why not? Quite a simple reason. For all his scientific genius, he didn't happen to notice that the baby had been playing on the floor and had pulled out the electric plug.

Isn't that our situation in the world today?

The electric plug amounts to practically nothing. It's just a tiny little thing, quite insignificant in comparison with the colossal cost of the wonderful machine itself. But little though the plug may be, if it isn't pushed into the current, there's no current, and the most magnificent apparatus on earth is good for nothing but to be broken up.

THE PRESENCE OF LOVE

What is this electric plug?

Not the kind of welfare-work which takes a benevolent interest in distress from the outside. It is the presence of people, working in groups and with that independent autonomy of which I spoke before, who go and incarnate themselves in the midst of suffering so as to give it a voice, so as to be able to harass the authorities and to explain the exact nature of the desperate necessity where help is needed.

And finally I said: It isn't your money which the world needs.

What the world needs is to know whether you are capable of giving the love of a human heart; whether your people is capable of producing boys and girls willing to come with empty hands and empty pockets, without dollars or money or cheque-books, to share in the suffering of those who, after all, if we really look at it—we, the people of Europe, have the right to say this—are in their present distress only because they have twice in forty years sacrificed the best part of their time, their youth and their wealth to defend *your* liberty and *your* opportunity to develop your powers.

There is no regret for what we had to undergo. There is no regret for the sacrifices made. But, in virtue of these sacrifices we have the right to speak with our heads up, and not to see ourselves always as clients and beggars; for the truth is that, in a certain sense, we started as creditors.

I may say in passing that it has happened several times that in religious circles people say to me, "Poor Father, how we admire you, but how sad it must be for you to live in that dreadful Communist country, when it is so atheist and so absolutely degenerate, and none of the young people have any ideals any more! How splendid it is of you!" And sometimes, when I had got a bit too irritated by the way this talk went on, I used to say to these fellow-priests: "How right you are! Yes indeed, France is a frightfully depraved country, frightfully decadent; no doubt your own spiritual values are incomparably higher. But—do excuse my ignorance—I should be very grateful if, for the record, you would let me have a list of your saints of the last hundred years, to compare with the list for France."

It's true that we are a poor lot from many points of view; we know it, and there is no need to tell us; but it is also true that there are some values and some fine things about us. We shall always be extremists, both for good and for ill; but what is absolutely necessary is that we should be capable of talking like this, with liberty and with pride. Furthermore, this is the proof of it: whenever anyone does take the risk, they appreciate it; they prefer people who talk like this to those who come slinking up to them perpetually in the guise of humble clients.

So, I said to them, this is what we have come to say. Your money will keep till later. It will be needed. It will quite certainly be needed, and you owe it to the world and have no right to waste it. You have been taught that, for the sake of national prosperity, it would be a crime to restrict expenditure.

You have been inculcated with the idea of thrift as a crime. Now, that makes sense for the New Deal period after the great Depression, a period when you were not involved in the international situation. But today you no longer have the right to live by this idea that it is a crime for an American citizen to economise. You ought to replace this idea of the crime of economy—the idea that it is a duty always to spend everything you've got, and even more by always living on credit—with the idea that extravagance is a crime in face of a world in which so many millions lack the bare necessities.

THE CRIME OF EXTRAVAGANCE

What you need to realise is that the demand now being made of you—and if you fail to meet it, you will perish, despite your material resources—is really a demand for a consciousness of solidarity, and a solidarity primarily in terms of the heart and of the human approach.

Look at the countries where you have gone—whether South America or Africa or Asia, or even to some extent Europe. If you start by arriving with plenty of money, what happens? I think it is mere honesty to say this. It is the most corrupt individuals in each nation whom you will see rushing up to you and kissing your hands. It is they who will come and slobber over you and fish in your pockets for dollars, while anyone who has any dignity will hold back for a while to see what manner of men you may be and what value your action has.

And because it is these, the most corrupt, who come first to flatter you and skilfully play on you in such terms as fit in best with your own preoccupations—for they will have studied them—you think that it is they who deserve your confidence. So it is to them that you entrust the utilisation of what you place at the disposal of these suffering nations, and because they are utterly corrupt it simply gets embezzled, and contributes only to fostering revolt and disgust and anger amongst the people.

What is needed is that before your money even arrives there should be generous human beings, simply as such, coming to live with those who are suffering.

If you are able to do this, then we may allow ourselves to hope for great things; for then this vast material power which circumstances have built up in your hands will cease to be a source of corruption and may become something fruitful.

2. WHAT WAS THEIR RESPONSE?

My answer to this is that it manifested itself in two main characteristics.

I went to the United States five or six years ago. What struck me enormously then was that the American subconscious mind was dominated by one very simple but very deep emotion. It has not been much spoken of, but I am sure that serious and perspicacious historians of a future age will focus upon this period in the soul of the American people—a time when it was dominated by a terrible, though confused and indefinable, sense of guilt; a bad conscience over the use of atomic weapons at the end of the war.

They did not talk about it, but if by chance, in intimate conversation, whether with distinguished or simple people, we touched on this subject, you could feel that here was something which really dominated the conscience of a whole nation.

There was a sort of sense of contrition prompting people to say: But the people who did it weren't pirates or gangsters; it wasn't the enemy, it wasn't our opponents, it was an ordinary American, a decent man, one of our statesmen who was capable of taking a decision like that, in cold blood; of thinking, at a given moment, that it was his duty. It wasn't that they blamed him, but they were desperately unhappy; and the result was a sort of moral complex in the whole nation which was extremely curious to observe.

It did not last long, because, with the usual instability of mass currents of opinion in that great nation, as soon as the news broke that the power confronting them disposed of the same force as themselves, this feeling underwent a transformation. It became a feeling of fear and insecurity, a feeling of the necessity for defence and precautions. At the political level, this took the form of a quite intelligible reaction—we should understand it perfectly if we would apply collective psychoanalysis—which gave birth to effects which we, from our point of view in Europe, thought incomprehensible and monstrous; they have now died down.

This time, I found neither of these two deep emotions. But I found two others which seemed to me to be very generally present in the American soul at this moment.

GOOD WILL

The first is an extraordinary feeling, such as I think I have not found anywhere in the world in the same degree—and I have visited a good many countries in the last ten years. It is what I may call the feeling of good will.

To simplify it, I might say that the thing I heard said most often, all up and down the social scale, amounted roughly to this: "Who will tell us what we must do in order to do good?" It is a sort of open availability, and a longing to serve. It is a sense of vast responsibility; the conscience of a spoilt child with a heart of gold called upon to pay huge, colossal taxes. This is something of which we have no idea. I am going to stick my neck out and say that people who break windows here because they think themselves overtaxed would, if they knew what goes on on the other side of the ocean, realise that over there they are regarded with crushing contempt, being looked on as people incapable of assuming their true responsibilities in the interests of the nation.

They bear these crushing charges; yet in spite of that their standard of living is higher than that of anyone else in the world; but they are all ready to do even better.

The second feeling—and this is the point at which I, personally, began to feel hope—is something confused but very general. It is a sense of humiliation arising out of the fact that, for the first time in its existence, this nation is deliberately trying to apply itself, steadily and on a larger scale, to outside problems, not its own; it is the first time that it is trying both to make itself known and to make itself loved through the services it is rendering, and it is the first time in its history that it is recognising its own power as powerless. Over and over again I heard them say, "But, Father, tell us why the more we give the more they hate us." It is a feeling which goes very deep in the hearts of all these men and women, both ordinary people and, in many cases, those in command. They say: "But why doesn't it work? Here are all the dodges and methods and techniques which have always worked extraordinarily efficiently in solving our own problems at home, and as soon as we get them transferred to outside problems, their results are always poor and sometimes catastrophic."

Hence a feeling of confusion and a sort of humiliation. This is a fresh phenomenon, additional to that of general good will.

THE MESSAGE OF EMMAUS

Then I tried to give them our message. This was what I said at San Francisco, the last city of the United States in which I spoke at a large public meeting. In that astonishing town, where you feel you have got into the south of France, there is a sort of Mediterranean psychology; people wear their hearts on their sleeves, and I did really find a particularly generous and understanding atmosphere.

In that town of San Francisco, which is called after St. Francis of Assisi, where my long journey—long in mileage, that is—came to an end, I summed up, in a fashion, the message I had tried to give in the name of the ragpickers of France, and all the poor folk who are worst off. In that town, ten years ago, in an access of somewhat naive hope (but nations, fortunately, do retain these naiveties and something of the freshness of children) the United Nations Charter was signed; and in that town, about now, the nations who signed it are to meet again. I said that it seems to me that we can definitely affirm that the future of the world depends above all on whether those who dispose of wealth and power, and especially you Americans, can be quick enough in producing your 1955 version of St. Francis of Assisi.

I have been told (I don't know whether or not it is true,

and I should be much interested if the Soviet citizens who are here this evening would give me the precise facts) that when Lenin was dying he said: "What we really needed at the heart of our revolutionary action was a complementary action like that of St. Francis of Assisi." I do not know whether this is true, but even if it was not said it is valid; it is true of every country in the world which possesses great power. It is true of America as I saw it, and I am certain that it is true of the Soviet Union and of the whole of Asia.

If the great powers are not capable of understanding quickly enough that technique, money and material resources ought to be, not abjured or destroyed or abandoned, but subordinated to man, then they will be destructive.

One day—it was in October a year and a half ago—I was invited to a meeting where there was a considerable group of people with heavy financial responsibilities. They were worried about the housing problem. There were representatives from the Savings Bank, the building fund, and other organisations. The chairman of the meeting said roughly this: "Gentlemen, I have called this meeting because we are, in accordance with the law, investing thousands of millions of bonuses in the Savings Bank, and thousands of millions from other sources, in housing. Now, we have to admit that we only achieve quite ridiculous results; luxury apartments multiply, and we make practically no progress in solving the problem of popular housing. But here is a man who, with a few ragpicking friends, with funds represented by dustbins and hundred-franc notes (this was before February last year) has achieved, in proportion, infinitely more than we have. I thought we should ask him to come and talk to us, and tell us what he knows and what he sees."

The answer I gave them was one which, for me, has immense value, summing up so many things and dominating all human problems: the answer to this riddle of the helplessness of your large-scale measures and the power of our feeble measures is quite simple; it is that with all the money in the world you can never make men, whereas if you have men you can make anything, including whatever money you need.

Money is necessary, but if you don't have humanity first, it is an abomination.

This is the framework in which I travelled through that great country and saw its reactions. What were they? A reaction of good will and of confusion in face of their own powerlessness and of the spiritual, mystical message which I brought to these calculating, practical men.

The truth, and I must say it, is that the response was shattering. It was such that, after the first days, I was forced by the extent of the emotion which was sweeping over those young people, to have as my constant preoccupation not to arouse emotion but to damp down the fire. Mass movements being what they are over there, we were threatened by the frightful danger of having a thousand or two thousand or ten thousand letters, telephone calls and telegrams coming in next morning, from boys saying: "Father, you are right. We are at your disposal. Tell us what to do."

It was a great risk, but it was absolutely impossible for us to think of directing all these generous impulses and assigning them specific tasks. There would have been the risk of starting an emotional movement at the mercy of any little whipper-snapper who cared to cover it with ridicule, and so of blighting for the future all these generous impulses which had thus been moved and stirred up to offer themselves for service.

So much so that we had, almost from the beginning, to adopt a very cold-blooded attitude, reasoning almost in scientific fashion in demonstration of these things. I always finished by saying: "Just as I have not come to ask for money, so I have not come to found a great international movement with its headquarters in Paris or some other city. I have come, very humbly, like a man who has discovered a vaccine in his laboratory. And I have come quite simply to bring you this vaccine, this virus or antivirus, which will enable you to destroy, or to co-operate in destroying, social poliomyelitis. I have brought you a technique, a sort of penicillin for the problems of social life, in showing you the necessity of love and the giving of oneself *before* the giving of goods and money. I have come to tell you about this. As for the virus, you can have it free. Get to work with it. It is for you to do what you want with it, and to begin by setting your own house in order."

At Washington, that marvellous, glorious city, which is like a park, I had, the evening before, visited the hidden streets in which, as in the hidden streets of Paris, there are blacks and whites, Puerto Ricans and all sorts of unfortunates living in frightful conditions. And I said: "After visiting your night-refuges, which are so much more modern, so much glossier and more comfortable and better equipped than the wretched things we can manage in our communities, it wrung my heart to see the miserable, beaten expressions on the faces of the unfortunates whom you help in them, sitting there on the benches. And I couldn't help thinking at once of the proud, happy faces of those fine people at home who have rediscovered their whole lives as men and their self-respect because we appealed to them to put themselves at the service of all the other forms of suffering around them.

"When you meet our ragpickers, the friends in our communities of ragpickers and builders, you cannot help being overwhelmed by the peace and joy radiating from their faces because they are *not* objects of charity being helped by benefactors. They are friends to whom someone has come and said, 'Look at your mates suffering there beside you. I can't manage to help them any more on my own. Won't you come, not to be helped by me but to give me a hand with helping these mothers who haven't any houses?' "

We succeeded in sowing a certain number of seeds of this sort, which are now sprouting disruptively in some of these splendid welfare organisations. I have to say, in all frankness (for I get plenty of echoes via the press, and in my letters), that there have been some ructions over it. For it upsets the habits of some of the welfare committees, who find it quite bewildering to be deprived of their poor and to find the poor suddenly developing a taste for being each other's benefactors.

3. WHAT LESSONS ARE WE TO DRAW?

I now come to the last point which I promised you this evening. What lessons are we to draw with reference to our hopes and fears for the future, and what are our responsibilities?

The lessons to be drawn are, I think, quite clear, quite simple, and quite beautiful.

Whatever our sympathies, antipathies or preferences may be, no one can seriously imagine or suggest, here and now, that we can cope with the world's present crisis—the crisis of world poverty, of the danger to world equilibrium resulting from that poverty (without reckoning the despair engendered in the souls of those who suffer it but are no longer stupefied

by it, who are becoming aware that it is idiotic, seeing that
the modern world has the means, if it will, to give them the
relief to which they have a right)—no serious person, then,
faced with this reality, can still imagine that we can provide
effective solutions to it piecemeal and without a minimum of
unity and co-operation between nations.

It is certain that this co-operation must be established, and
that we must establish it first at a level which everyone has
forgotten.

DANGERS

I will now give you the lesson which I personally have
brought back with me, and which I pass on to you confiden-
tially so that you too can meditate upon it. I do so confi-
dentially only for the time being, until we set about making it
echo, with all the violence we can manage, across our country
and throughout the whole world.

These giant material forces, such as we can find in our
neighbours in America, are really a terrifying danger to the
world, because their power can swell any mistakes that may be
made to fantastic proportions. They will be a gigantic danger
unless the other nations, which are of course quite incapable
of claiming any equality with them in material or financial
power, older nations, nations which are bled white and exhausted like ours, wake up to their responsibilities in relation
to these material forces.

It is for us to give to the youth of America, with all their
good will, a humble and simple example of dignity, intelligence and human psychology, out of what has been given us

by our long past, our long ancestry, and all the mixture of elements in the crises of history which have made France what she is.

HOPE

If we are not capable of being humanly intelligent in this way, and of proving it within our own country and in our relations with neighbouring countries, then the dangers are great. But if we are capable, in dignity and pride, of at least beginning to solve our own problems with efficiency, intelligence and human realism, then we may have great hopes. For it is as false to suppose that the youth of America is incapable of understanding such an example of humanity as we should then be giving as it is false to suppose that the youth of France is incapable of giving it.

Eighteen months ago the people of France arose in an absolutely unpredictable, improbable, unplanned surge of action, by which we ourselves were the first to be submerged because we had never for a moment imagined anything like it. The people who tried, afterwards, as I read in some of the newspapers, to make out that it had all been planned and carried out by Heaven knows what cunning device are, quite simply, stupid. It was neither foreseen nor prepared. It was a cry which went up from some poor men who had been scavenging in muck for years and who launched that appeal on the 1st of February because they saw the growing crowds of people sleeping out of doors on the pavements. And the reason for *that* was that all the mass of people who normally sleep in cellars and attics preferred to come out and walk the streets, to stamp their feet or crouch over a warm ventilator, rather than risk dying of cold where they lay in their cellars. No one could have foreseen the consequences which were to follow.

Now, didn't what happened that day (and your presence here this evening, eighteen months later, is evidence of this) prove that it is not true that the people of France are incapable of generosity? It is those who have the task of governing them who are incapable of offering them tasks to match their generosity.

France has a wonderful mission and task before her still, which she must accomplish and which she is perfectly capable of accomplishing.

REAL BLASPHEMY

I finished my wanderings over the American continent in Catholic Canada—overwealthy Canada, though she too has her slums and her horrible examples of poverty. It was at a meeting on the hill of Mont-Royal at Montreal, before an audience of twenty thousand people, and I spoke, over the radio and television, words which seemed positively incendiary. The moment has come, I said, when those who claim to be Christians must awake to the fact that, in God's eyes, blasphemy does not lie in the angry cry which rises to a man's lips when he sees his children suffering. Nor does it lie in the cries of anger, despair or revolt which arise from a people who have for too long been subjected to exploitation. It lies in the indifference in the hearts of those who claim to be Christians to the profanation of the image of God which is happening in thousands of millions of human beings throughout the world.

Standing before a vast basilica for which they are collecting fantastic sums of money, I said: of course we need places of worship, of course we need places where we can meet together to pray; but, for mercy's sake, while you still have slums in your town, as soon as you have built the four walls and put on a roof, stop decorating your sanctuary and understand this (and let us all understand it, for we all need to examine our consciences in this matter): it is not in the Eucharist that Jesus is cold; it is not in piling gold and marble and sumptuous stuffs round Jesus in the Eucharist that we shall honour Him; it is in coming to His aid in the hands and feet of children throughout the world who are dying of cold because we have no care for them.

A NEW CRUSADE

Perhaps the hour has come when France—for she is certainly capable of it—is to launch a new crusade with that cry of "God wills it!" which I gave there at Montreal. The crusade which God wants of us today is not to go off and free the empty tomb where the Body of Our Lord once rested, but to build houses around the living sons of men who are sons of God. Such is the mission which has been imposed upon us.

Each of our parishes and schools ought to consider that it has not fulfilled its mission until the day when, instead of providing expensive decorations, it can pave the floor of the nave in the church or the hall in the school or the *mairie* with triumphant photographs of the slums it has cleared and the magnificent terraces of houses it has built for the people.

Such indeed is the task which we ought to accomplish today; but unless we are capable of giving our hearts as human beings, it will not be accomplished. If we wait for money to accomplish it, it will never be accomplished. Money will come. Enough will come, and perhaps far more than enough, once we have given our living hearts.

This evening, which is my first contact with all of you, the people of Paris, after my long absence throughout the winter, I want to give you a rendezvous for our future appeals; for our campaign to awaken the national conscience has not come to an end.

We are in grave danger from those who wield all the great material forces unless we are capable, through the way in which we solve our own domestic problems, of showing them the example of a great force of love. If we cannot give this example, then, no matter what military and material precautions we take, it will be those who are readier than we for sacrifice, despite the falsity of their materialist doctrine, who will inevitably be the final victors; for they will inevitably gain the day against those who have put their trust in what is sheer nothingness unless it is sustained and prepared by love; the nothingness which is matter and money.

Let us beware.

I am a spiritualist. I believe with all my soul, poor sinner that I am, and I desire to love with all my heart that Eternal Being of whom I believe that He is Someone, that He loves us, that we come from Him and are going to Him; but I sometimes tremble at the thought that those who pride themselves upon this doctrine of the spirit sometimes live more materialistically than those who, for their part, acknowledge only a materialist creed. And this is something which terrifies me.

The world is torn in two. It is torn in two in a fashion which fills us with terror for our children and for tomorrow. But do you not think that we can say quite truthfully that the split has come simply from one half of the world trying to rebuild the world by recovering that half of the Gospel which we Christians had thrown in the dustbin?

LIVING THE GOSPEL

If we were capable of reliving the Gospel whole and entire, of receiving it once more in its fullness by giving the whole of ourselves, what a number of equivocations would fade away! Of course many ideological and intellectual differences would remain; but the light would shine once more upon the great mass of generous souls thirsting for nourishment and justice and love. That is our task today.

It is for us, the people of France—after all, this is the meaning of democracy—to prove that we are capable of organising ourselves and demanding from those who govern us, whoever they may be, all the housing which we need.

Changing the ministers makes little difference. They are always changing, and housing never figures any more largely in the programme of the new one than in that of the last. What matters to us is not who is going to be the minister, today or tomorrow or the day after, but what programme he is going to propose. And when we look at these programmes side by side, we can observe that they have been repeating each other indefinitely over the last ten years and that they never amount to anything except a repetition of monstrosities of unrealism. We find them saying, "I'm going to be the most social-minded minister in the world. I won't have any more jerry-built houses. I won't have houses built at popular prices without such-and-such wonderful and magnificent comforts and improvements." May we be so tactless as to ask just how many of these high-class buildings you actually guarantee to complete? We are very strong on models in France, but we are never "in a position" to complete the project. Are they really resolved to produce these perfect, comfortable houses on a large scale? If so, we shall go along with them, with all our strength and energy. But it should be realised that if they do adopt this policy, as I hope with all my heart they may, we have no right to ignore the fact that whoever is in power —extreme Right or extreme Left—he won't be able to carry out this wonderful programme in less than a matter of years— three, five or perhaps ten. The Conseil Economique are talk- ing in terms of thirty years.

Are they just going to go on making speeches at us all that time, and refusing to have the courage to take the decisions which they only shrink from taking out of hypocrisy and pharisaism? I mean the decisions bound up with recognising that there are several hundreds of thousands of French work- ers, with their wives and families, now living in conditions fit only for animals, who will tomorrow be lunatics, alcoholics and delinquents, leaving us a trail of abandoned children and perhaps turning into gangsters because we have done nothing for them.

We must unite and demand that the long-term policy be combined with emergency measures.

THE LESSON OF THE EMMAUS RAGPICKERS

Every evening and every day we have mothers coming to us with their children. They've been turned out of their hotel room, they can't pay the rent any more. My comrades say, "Father, we can't cope, we just don't know where to put them." Of course, we do invent solutions; but are they going to go on indefinitely in this cowardly fashion—those who dis- pose of the nation's power, I mean—depending on ragpickers to look after all these cases of emergency hardship? In the last analysis, it's a swindle. Of course *we* are willing. We are more than willing to give everything we have. We only have our own two arms and our own strength and our own will to work. We aren't angels or saints. My comrades are no better than anyone else, but they rediscovered the joy of living on the day when they were told that the joy of living consists in helping first those who are suffering most. With all their faults, these men are giving the whole of society the fundamental lesson it needs.

But what can they do? There are eight hundred of them. They work and do what they can with their whole hearts, but does anyone imagine that *they* can solve the problem?

Because we weren't able to resume our campaign this winter with all the energy required—because of the months of organisation necessarily arising out of the events of last winter—we have had people pouring stories down our throats about a "revolution of charity." Today, I hold in my conscience as a man and a Christian, and I must proclaim it with all possible solemnity, that if there *was* a "revolution of charity," its time is past. It is no longer a question of charity; it is a question of establishing justice; if we don't, what we shall have is a revolution of fury.

MOBILISATION

We don't ask the impossible. All we ask is that they shall recognise the realities of the situation with a certain amount of frankness, and issue a decree mobilising the resources of the nation; for nothing less than such a mobilisation can measure up to France's present housing crisis.

Suppose we had a war tomorrow. Suppose we had it in

what I would, if the phrase were not a monstrosity, call "perfect conditions"; conditions in which there were no divisions of opinion amongst the people of France—an invasion of Martians, for instance—and that the whole nation, as one man, decided to fight. Within twenty-four hours we should have found whatever financial measures, supplies of raw materials, skilled labour and factories were needed to produce tanks, planes and munitions, deliver them free of charge and hurl them against the enemy. No modern nation of any industrial capacity has been known to say, "Count me out. I won't go to war because I haven't got the materials or the man-power and I can't solve my armaments problems."

Do they really think that we are stupid enough to believe or admit that, now that the war is over and it is no longer a question of defending freedom, we simply haven't got the financial and technical means and the man-power to save the lives of hundreds of thousands of the children of France? If we have the means in war-time, then we have the same means in peace-time, for saving the lives of the nation's children—if the nation wants to live. If she wants not to be contemptible, then she must prove herself capable of demanding this much from those who govern her, whoever they may be: mobilisation, the requisition of land, and the decrees needed to call up volunteers, if there are enough, and—why not?—if there aren't, then a real mobilisation of manpower so as to get work started everywhere.

We can do it if we want to.

Last year Germany built 540,000 homes, whereas we only built 150,000. Are we supposed to think that we aren't as clever as they?

Ten days ago, I paid a visit to one of the highest officials of the Paris district. I was, by the way, delighted to find him a human, understanding person. I told him that the situation is such that when people come and say to me, "Monsieur l'Abbé, such and such of your activities don't keep within the law," I answer—and I wanted him to know this, as I might have occasion to say it to him more than once—"Are the things I am doing necessary in order to save lives, or not? If they are not necessary, prove it. But if you can't prove that they are unnecessary, then you must recognise that it is your laws which are illegal, because they are inhuman."

ALLIANCE FOR BUILDING

They talk about Europe. How often I have said to my friends in Parliament or in the Government: "If you had any understanding whatever of the soul of the people, you wouldn't have founded this Europe of yours (which is a highly desirable thing, regarded as a loosening of frontiers, a widening of the scope of economic life, and a better understanding of the psychology of our neighbours)—you wouldn't have founded it on technical mysteries like the coal and steel pool, or things which are revolting to people's feelings, like the re-armament plan; you would have founded it on an alliance for building. And Europe would have come into being, for the youth of all nations would have united in love in order to build and house and save the families which have been visited by the horrors of war."

Of course I thoroughly believe that the problem is a political one; it needs to be solved at the political, administrative, technical level, true; it depends on international reconciliation, true; but it is primarily a human problem, a problem of love and of the human approach, a question of reproducing everywhere that kind of leaven which has been introduced into the nation by communities like the one which we have tried to fashion.

And now, with my whole heart and soul, I am making a most ardent appeal. I wish it to be heard by the whole of France.

The Emmaus Brotherhood is coming into being. Its novitiate is being set up formally and officially in October, to provide monks who are missionaries of poverty, monks dedicated to building. We must have vocations. We must have boys whose hearts prompt them to come and say, "Father, I want to try and see if I can do it."

And along with this little nucleus of men dedicated, heart and soul, to communion with suffering, so as to be able to give it a resounding voice capable of penetrating even as far as those who govern us, we need temporary volunteers to join the sort of Foreign Legion for peace of which our communities are already, basically, a kind of prototype.

Among our eight hundred comrades there are ten, twelve or fifteen who are there because of the mystique of a spiritual vocation to give their lives in this way. And there are eight hundred who are there because they were struck down by misfortune and then rediscovered joy in this sort of Foreign Legion where they give their whole hearts, not to military combat but to building.

When I saw the President of the United States I gave him a copy of *Abbé Pierre and the Ragpickers,** after writing a dedication in it. I was thinking, very sadly, of a day which is now no more than a bad memory and which we hope to forget, when the man who was to become the President of that great

---

* By Boris Simon: London, Harvill Press; New York, Kenedy.

nation said, without thinking, that the moral fibre of the
French people was so totally decayed that nothing could be
expected of it. So I wrote this dedication: "I present to you
these pages of history and humanity, of suffering and love,
about the volunteers who fought a peace-time battle. If we are
not able to ask as much heroism of our youth in time of peace
as we asked them to give in the war in defence of an imperfect
freedom, if we cannot ask them to be ready to die, if need be,
in order to house and feed and teach and care for those who
are in desperate need, then it was not worth asking them to
die for freedom. God grant that you may be able to arouse the
hearts of many of your people to such generosity as this."

Such is the appeal that I am making to you now.

Besides those who consecrate their whole lives as monks, we
need young men willing to give us six months or a year of
their lives (not a week; that's worth nothing, except in snob-
value): volunteers coming to share in the fight with us, so
that, in every town of France, we shall be able to gather the
desperate people and say: "Come. Do you want to join a community and build houses for the homeless? Do you want to go
to North Africa?" For we shall be going to do something in
those towns over there where tragedy is so imminent and
where it may be that before long suffering will be sweeping
not only over us but over those other peoples, in consequence
of the growing lack of understanding.

VOLUNTARY SERVICE

We need young men capable of understanding all this. They
accept military service. They rationalise it, but yet they know

that if all goes well it will be completely wasted, and if it is needed that will be the end of everything. Yet they accept it as something necessary and do it.

Can't we be sufficiently intelligent, clearheaded and generous to be ready, with our education behind us and before we begin to make money, to volunteer to give six months or a year of our lives, not for something which we hope is going to be useless, but for a task which means that when we lie down at night, dead beat, each one of us can think of how he built a wall or put on a roof or made some contribution to a home; so that—as it will be at Boulogne on Sunday, thanks to the work, and exhaustion, and privation of some of our comrades —they can have the joy of seeing four, five or six mothers come to them with their children and say, "Thank you; you have saved us."

Shall we not find boys in France willing to come and cooperate with us in gathering together those whom people call tramps? There are so many among them who only ask one thing: to be offered the possibility of doing something useful of which they can see the use, and not just to enrich a set of anonymous shareholders. When they have lost their wife and children and home in the war, or through captivity, or if, after committing some crime and being in prison, the hypocrisy of our society excludes them wherever they turn, they have no heart for anything any more. There are thousands and thousands of them.

Won't the youth of France produce such an array of volunteers as to make it possible for us to go not merely from two hundred to eight hundred, as we did last year, but from eight hundred to two thousand, or even eight thousand in a year or two? All the towns of France are appealing to us for men capable of transforming the town into a living, redemptive community, a community able, by the work it is doing, to present a challenge to the whole of society and to the public authorities.

This is my appeal. May all the youth of France show itself able to respond!

There are young Americans and Canadians who are going to cross the sea in a few days' time, on July 1st, to come and work in obscurity with us on rubbish heaps so as to spend a few weeks learning what they have already understood. Then they will go home and begin, in their own towns, to gather desperate people and down-and-outs together, and re-live the adventure of Emmaus in their own countries.

Surely we are going to find the necessary response amongst ourselves?

There are those of you who can become neither monks of poverty nor temporary volunteers giving six months or a year of their youth to supply a core of generosity amongst our comrades, and to learn to love man by seeing him in the nakedness both of his suffering and of his courage. All the rest of you, who have other obligations and vocations, who are fathers and mothers, perhaps, bound to other tasks, do not think that I am going to let you off! You cannot be monks of poverty, you cannot belong to the Foreign Legion of peace; then be active members of your action committee for aid to the homeless.

Join the committee in your own district, as you were asked to do just now by M. Croué, the president of the Paris association for aid to the homeless. And, as you go out, you'll be offered a dustbin: put what you can into it.

At Noisy-le-Grand we still have forty families in tents. We need two hundred thousand francs for each family to provide them with a fibro-cement hut. We have already built two hun-

dred of them entirely on our own. And there is a constant
stream of families begging us to take them in.

Last week, as you know, a tent caught fire and two children
were burnt alive. You could perhaps have a tragedy like that
anywhere when a child does something foolish; but it is much
more horrible when you see it happening under such conditions.

Remember that if we have fifty such families on our hands,
there are fifty thousand of them throughout France. They will
be turning into broken homes, girls on the streets, men becoming criminals, children on public assistance, if we don't, within
a year or so, give them some emergency help in the shape of
the huts we can provide with the money you give us and,
especially, with the strong arms and hearts which the young
men are going to bring to their aid.

They will be holding out dustbins to you. Put in your
money and your jewellery. We have just been selling some for
more than two million francs. I brought it back from the
United States. Even when I was on the boat people were
secretly bringing me more; I found it on the table in my
cabin. Give what you can.

If you want God to bless your children, think of those who
are under a curse because of our indifference.

Put your visiting card into the dustbins, too. Put on your
name, address, telephone number and profession. If you prefer,
write to us—"Abbé Pierre, Paris." That's enough, because the
Post Office is very much on the spot, and letters do get to us.

Thus our committees will grow into a force spreading from
district to district. And if some day—after all, why not?—we
get so desperate that we have to decide to put squatters into
some block of flats (for there are some, with room for two
hundred or five hundred families, standing empty indefinitely),

we shall be able, having committees everywhere, to move in not just with forty of our comrades from the communities but with forty thousand citizens of Paris to see these hundreds of families into their home.

And finally, when each of you has given as much as he can —as monks of poverty, or temporary volunteers, or just as members of the committees for aid to the homeless—when you have given us your lives and your goods, take out a subscription to the review *Faim et Soif* of which they are showing you copies. It has fifty thousand subscribers already, but it must have countless more. Help us to produce it. It has got to become an organ—not of violence in any malicious sense, but of violence according to the mind of God: I mean that it must be able, like the very heart of God, to give a voice, in hunger and thirst after justice, to what I will call the wrath of love.